THE BEST
High/Low Books for Reluctant Readers

Libraries Unlimited Data Books

American History for Children and Young Adults: An Annotated Bibliographic Index. By Vandelia VanMeter.

The Best: High/Low Books for Reluctant Readers. By Marianne Laino Pilla.

CD-ROM: An Annotated Bibliography. By Ahmed M. Elshami.

Science Experiments Index for Young People. By Mary Anne Pilger.

THE BEST
High/Low Books for Reluctant Readers

MARIANNE LAINO PILLA

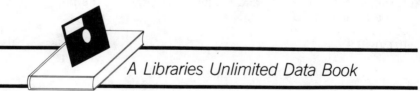

A Libraries Unlimited Data Book

1990
LIBRARIES UNLIMITED, INC.
Englewood, Colorado

LIBRARIES UNLIMITED, INC.
P.O. Box 3988
Englewood, CO 80155-3988

Library of Congress Cataloging-in-Publication Data

Pilla, Marianne Laino, 1955-
    The best : high/low books for reluctant readers / Marianne Laino
Pilla.
      xv, 100 p. 22x28 cm. -- (A Libraries Unlimited data book)
      ISBN 0-87287-532-6
      1. High interest-low vocabulary books--Bibliography.   2. Slow
learning children--Books and reading.   I. Title.   II. Series:
Libraries Unlimited data books.
    Z1039.S5P53   1990
    016.0285'35--dc20   90-5756
                                                             CIP

For Lou

Contents

Libraries Unlimited Data Books

The Libraries Unlimited Data Book series consists of bibliographies and indexes that are issued simultaneously in traditional print format and in one or several computerized databases. Unlike most CD-ROM products, data books are designed as inexpensive in-house resources to be used with popular database managers used by most libraries, such as Microsoft Works, AppleWorks, or dBase.

Indexes presented in the series provide an innovative idea in indexing for the individual library. Purchasers can tailor the index to their own collections. For example, if the database indexes 300 books and the library owns only 200 of those titles, the 100 titles not owned by the library can be deleted from the database, thus producing an index that matches the library's collection. Titles owned by the library but not indexed can be added to the database as needed. The database can be printed out or consulted by computer as needed by library patrons.

Bibliographies in the series have the advantage of being searched in ways not possible with the printed version. The limitations of these searches are those of the database manager that the librarian uses, that is, the limitations are those of dBase III +, PC File +, Microsoft Works, or any other package used to search the data. The advantage of the bibliography on disk is that it can be modified to suit the needs of local patrons. Local call numbers may be added, new entries may be added by the library, and the publisher can keep the bibliography current between editions of the printed version. Versions for IBM, Macintosh, and the Apple II family are available. Write or call the publisher for details.

Special Needs

Libraries or individuals needing the data in a special computer format or needing parts of the databases are invited to write to the editorial department of Libraries Unlimited for assistance. Include a description of your needs and the format in which you wish the data to be arranged. A price quotation will be provided by return mail.

Users who find errors in the data or who could provide updates to the data are invited to correspond with the editorial department.

Write:

Head, Editorial Department
Libraries Unlimited, Inc.
P.O. Box 3988
Englewood, CO 80155-3988
Phone: (303) 770-1220

Acknowledgments

My gratitude to the following librarians from the Free Library of Phila-delphia — Hedra Peterman and Lois Hartman, children's librarians; Anita Winston, young adult librarian; Kit Breckinridge from the Office of Work with Children; and Vicki Collins, in Reader Development — for sharing all of their expertise and good new books with me. Thank you also to Carolyn Walsh and Barbara Daebeler, from Villanova University's Library Science Department, for allowing me to camp out in their library with their new books; to Margery Hall at Ludington Public Library, for "hunting and fetching"; to Ellen LiBretto, for her suggestions and encouragement; to my editor, David V. Loertscher, for his calm and reassuring nature; and to his assistant, Susie Sigman, for her cheerfulness; and to my husband, Lou, for his unwavering patience, understanding, and computer expertise.

Introduction

The purpose of this bibliography is to provide a list of quality, easy-to-read, low-vocabulary books for librarians, teachers, parents, or tutors to recommend to reluctant readers in grades 3-12, primarily for recreational purposes. Of course, this does not exclude the use of these titles for classroom discussion or for tutoring. But these books were selected mostly to entice the poor or reluctant reader to spend more time enjoying reading as a leisurely, pleasurable activity.

Reluctant readers are defined as those who usually read two or more levels below their grade levels. It also applies, in some cases, to those who can read on their level but who choose not to. However, generally, the books were selected with poor readers in mind.

I have chosen to keep the designation "high interest/low vocabulary" because it still continues to best identify those books for reluctant readers that have low or relatively low reading levels. And I believe that many professionals still refer to these materials as "hi/lo" or variations thereof.

Librarians, teachers, and parents will find approximate reading levels useful when selecting books for reluctant readers. Therefore, reading levels are included in this bibliography despite current trends to omit them.

I have applied the Fry Readability Scale (Extended) to assign a reading level to each work. Exceptions are the poetry and joke books that are difficult to gauge because they do not use sentences. In these cases, the reading level is indicated as "varies." The reading level given is an approximation. It is important for the user to work with the reader's needs and interests when recommending titles.

All of the books included have been carefully examined for content appeal, art work, format, reading level, typeface and leading (amount of space between lines). Barbara Bates's "Quick Evaluation: Hi/Low Book"[1] was used to evaluate titles for this bibliography.

Many of the titles have been recommended by reading professionals and children's librarians and have appeared in published lists such as *Choices*[2] *and High Interest Easy Reading for Junior and Senior High School Students*,[3] Ellen LiBretto's *High/Low Handbook*,[4] and the Young Adult Services Division's "Recommended Books for the Reluctant Young Adult Reader, 1988."[5]

However, I have personally reevaluated each book for relevancy based on Bates's evaluative criteria. I found many of the titles included in the previously published lists had reading levels much above the traditional level of two or more below the child's grade level. Even though they were good stories, they were too challenging (e.g., *Julie of the Wolves*), so they were not included in this list. Several titles are my own choices based on nearly a decade of selecting and recommending books as a children's librarian in public libraries.

I have tried to cover as many subject areas as possible. There is a need for more books that meet the qualifications of quality literature with both high appeal as well as low vocabulary for the reluctant reader, especially in the sports biography area.

The Best: High/Low Books for Reluctant Readers is an attempt to fill the void of up-to-date guides to recreational books that both exhibit good qualities and meet the variety of reading needs and interests of reluctant readers. The use of the word *best* is intended to mean the best of what is available, past and present. I attempted to include books of the finest quality. But in keeping the reader and his or her interests in mind, some popular works that may not meet strict criteria by professional standards have been included.

Date of publication was *not* a criteria in choosing the books for this list. Old, out-of-print favorites, many that are still found on library shelves, have been included so professionals may make the best use of the resources on hand. Some have been reprinted as paperbacks; some may be reprinted in the future. In addition, the newest titles from 1988 and 1989 are included.

Each entry includes complete bibliographic information including ISBNs, out-of-print status (designated "OP"), a brief annotation, subject headings, and reading and interest levels.

An additional feature of the Databook series is that this entire book is available as a database for Apple (AppleWorks), Macintosh (Microsoft Works), and IBM (comma delimited ASCII files). The database version can be obtained from the publisher and is very useful in adding titles, deleting titles, adding local call numbers, printing out reading lists, and ordering titles in the list. Contact the publisher for further information.

NOTES

[1]Barbara Bates. "Quick Evaluation: Hi/Low Book." in Marianne Laino Pilla. *Resources for Middle-Grade Reluctant Readers: A Guide for Librarians* (Littleton, Colo.: Libraries Unlimited, 1987), p. 37.

[2]Carolyn Sherwood Flemming, ed. *Choices: A Core Collection for Young Reluctant Readers.* Vol. 1. (Evanston, Ill.: John Gordon Burke Publisher, 1983).

[3]National Council of Teachers of English. *High Interest Easy Reading for Junior and Senior High School Students.* 5th ed. (Urbana, Ill.: NCTE, 1988).

[4]Ellen LiBretto. *High/Low Handbook* (New York: R. R. Bowker, 1985).

[5]Young Adult Services Division, American Library Association. "Recommended Books for the Reluctant Young Adult Reader, 1988." *Booklist* (April 15, 1988): 1420-22. _____. "Recommended for Reluctant YA Readers." *School Library Journal* 35 (March 1989): 99.

Key to Abbreviations

GrL   Grade level

LB   Library bind edition

OP   Out of print

PB   Paperback edition

RdL   Reading level

Alphabetical Listing of Authors

1. Aaseng, Nathan. **Baseball: It's Your Team**. Dell, 1985.
    103 p. ISBN: 0-440-90507-9 PB; GrL: 6-up; RdL: 7
    Ten true-to-life situations affecting major-league baseball team owners. The
    reader is invited to make management decisions by reading the facts. With
    black-and-white photographs.

2. Aaseng, Nathan. **Football: It's Your Team**. Dell, 1985.
    102 p. ISBN: 0-440-92648-3 PB; GrL: 6-up; RdL: 7
    Similar in format and theme to Aaseng's Baseball: It's Your Team. The
    reader participates in management decisionmaking by reading facts and
    making choices. With black-and-white photographs.

3. Abels, Harriet Sheffer. **Haunted Motorcycle Shop**. Childrens Press, 1978.
    45 p. ISBN: 0-516-03488-X; GrL: 5-8; RdL: 3; OP
    Eerie events in a motorcycle repair shop stun Chuck Walters and his
    friends—tools fly and a creepy coldness fills the garage. The mystery
    involves the ghost of a suicide victim from the past.

4. Adams, Barbara Johnston. **Picture Life of Bill Cosby**. Franklin Watts,
    1986.
    47 p. ISBN: 0-531-10168-1; GrL: 4-6; RdL: 3
    The life and career of this popular television comedian is told in simple,
    large type, from his childhood in Philadelphia to his successful television
    show. Black-and-white photographs accompany this book, which empha-
    sizes going after what you want and succeeding.

5. Adler, C.S. **Split Sisters**. Macmillan, 1986.
    161 p. ISBN: 0-02-700380-9; GrL: 5-up; RdL: 5
    Eleven-year-old Case schemes to keep her family together after her parents
    decide to separate. Now she and her sister must live apart. But in the process
    a young girl gives up her selfishness and learns the true meaning of family.

6. Adler, David A. **Cam Jansen & the Mystery of the Stolen Diamonds**.
    Viking (Cam Jansen Adventure Series), 1980.
    64 p. ISBN: 0-670-20039-5; GrL: 2-4; RdL: 2
    Cam Jansen, a young female sleuth, uses her photographic mind to capture a
    group of jewelry thieves. There are eight others in this popular, easy-to-read
    series. The large print and black-and-white sketches are similar to the
    Fourth Floor Twins series by Adler.

7. Adler, David A. **Dinosaur Princess and Other Prehistoric Riddles**. Holiday House, 1988.
    n.p. ISBN: 0-8234-0686-5; GrL: 2-5; RdL: 2
    Over 50 riddles about every dinosaur imaginable and more. With big illustrations accompanying one riddle per page.

8. Adler, David A. **Fourth Floor Twins and the Sand Castle Contest**. Viking, 1988.
    n.p. ISBN: 0-670-82150-0; GrL: 2-4; RdL: 2
    Sixth in this popular series featuring two sets of twins who live in the same apartment complex and who solve mysteries together. The first in the series is The Fourth Floor Twins and the Fish Snitch Mystery.

9. Adler, David A. **Jeffrey's Ghost and the Fifth-Grade Dragon**. Holt, Rinehart and Winston, 1985.
    52 p. ISBN: 0-03-069281-4; GrL: 3-5; RdL: 2
    A 200-year-old ghost named Bradford lives in Jeffrey's new house and makes attendance in his new school difficult for Jeffrey. But the spectre redeems himself by helping Jeffrey with a school project about what it was like for a student 200 years ago.

10. Adoff, Arnold. **Malcolm X**. Thomas Y. Crowell, 1970.
    41 p. ISBN: 0-690-51414-X LB; 0-690-51415-8 PB; GrL: 3-6; RdL: 3; OP
    Story of the famous black American spokesman who made black people proud of their heritage and was assassinated because of it. It tells of his hard childhood and how he rose from a life of crime to become one of the most outspoken and respected men of his time.

11. Alexander, Sue. **Finding Your First Job**. E.P. Dutton, 1980.
    73 p. ISBN: 0-525-29725-1; 0-525-45049-1 PB; GrL: 9-up; RdL: 3
    Tells how to determine a suitable job, where to look for it, how to apply and interview. Includes sample employment applications.

12. Ames, Lee J. **Draw Fifty Monsters, Creeps, Superheroes, etc**. Doubleday, 1983.
    64 p. ISBN: 0-385-17638-4 LB; 0-385-17639-2 PB; GrL: 4-up; RdL: no words
    This series is appropriate for the nonreader who likes to draw, since the books are wordless. Step-by-step drawings from basic sketches to the finished product show how to draw these popular figures. Others in the series include automobiles, airplanes, cartoons and other subjects of interest.

13. Anderson, LaVere. **Mary McLeod Bethune: Teacher with a Dream**. Garrard, 1976.
    80 p. ISBN: 0-8116-6321-3; GrL: 3-5; RdL: 3; OP
    The moving biography of a black woman born in 1875 into a poor family and her education against great odds. With determination and faith, she became a teacher with a mission. She elevated the black community of Daytona, Florida, with her school for black girls and taught the adults practical trades.

14. Angell, Judie. **Dear Lola or How to Build Your Own Family**. Bradbury Press, 1980.
    166 p. ISBN: 0-87888-170-0; GrL: 4-6; RdL: 4
    Annie tells how she and an unusual group of foster children escape their institution and look for a home of their own. They are led by a teenager, "Lola," who writes a newspaper column. All is well until the neighbors start to notice the clear absence of parents in their house.

15. Anonymous. **Go Ask Alice**. Avon, 1982.
    189 p. ISBN: 0-380-00523-9; GrL: 7-up; RdL: 4
    Gripping diary of a 15-year-old drug addict revealing her innermost thoughts. A powerful, graphic expose of her loneliness, escape into drugs and her eventual downward slide.

16. Appel, Marty. **First Book of Baseball**. Crown Publishers, Inc., 1988.
    95 p. ISBN: 0-517-56726-1; GrL: 2-6; RdL: 4
    This introduction to baseball features the history, techniques, how to understand and keep baseball statistics and scores, events during the baseball season and a section on baseball cards.

17. Arnosky, Jim. **Gray Boy**. Lothrop, Lee & Shepard, 1988.
    82 p. ISBN: 0-688-07345-X; GrL: 6-8; RdL: 5
    Thirteen-year-old Ian Emerson was given a dog, Gray Boy, the last gift from his father before he died. Despite Ian's efforts to tame the dog, he realizes he must let Gray Boy go back into the wilderness as the dog's behavior worsens. Ian encounters the dog one last time in a heartbreaking scene when Gray Boy saves his life.

18. Arrick, Fran. **Chernowitz!** New American Library (Signet Vista), 1981.
    183 p. ISBN: 0-451-12286-0; GrL: 6-up; RdL: 5
    When 15-year-old Bobby Cherno is harassed by a group of prejudiced classmates, he plans his revenge. But in doing so learns that his way is just as bad and the only way to combat ignorance is through education.

19. Avi. **Bright Shadow**. Bradbury Press, 1985.
    167 p. ISBN: 0-02-707750-0; GrL: 5-9; RdL: 2
    Morwenna, a 12-year-old maiden, inherits a dying wizard's magic wishes. She must keep this a secret, but she uses these wishes to save her people's kingdom from a tyrant ruler who wants to possess this magic.

20.   Avi. **Devil's Race**. Flare, 1987.
118 p. ISBN: 0-380-70406-4 PB; GrL: 6-up; RdL: 2
A graveyard meeting is John Proud's first encounter with his family's link to an evil ancestor. As he tries to fight this demon, he succumbs to the terrifying reality that this evil is taking over his soul and his body as he gradually weakens.

21.   Avi. **Man from the Sky**. Alfred A. Knopf, 1980.
117 p. ISBN: 0-394-94468-2; 0-394-84468-8 PB; GrL: 4-6; RdL: 2
A thief jumps off a plane with one million dollars and a parachute in an almost foolproof plan. But he doesn't count on being spotted by a boy who spends his time "reading the sky." The boy has a reputation for making up stories, so there is conflict when people don't believe his account of a falling man.

22.   Avi. **No More Magic**. Pantheon, 1975.
138 p. ISBN: 0-394-83084-9; 0-394-93084-3 LB; GrL: 3-6; RdL: 3; OP
While searching for his bicycle that disappeared on Halloween night, a young boy and his friends become involved in a magic adventure as strange things begin to happen.

23.   Avi. **Romeo and Juliet: Together (and Alive) at Last**. Orchard (Watts), 1987.
122 p. ISBN: 0-531-05721-6 TR; 0-531-08321-7 LB; GrL: 5-8; RdL: 2
An eighth-grade class stages the play Romeo and Juliet, so they can bring two shy classmates who like each other together. Ed Sitrow tells the funny story of the budding romance of his two friends, the stars, and the unexpected results that follow.

24.   Avi. **Wolf Rider: A Tale of Terror**. Bradbury Press, 1986.
202 p. ISBN: 0-02-707760-8; GrL: 7-up; RdL: 3
After receiving an apparent crank call from a man claiming to have murdered a college coed, Andy finds his once-close relationship with his widowed father crumbles. He tries to solve the mystery so everyone will believe him.

25.   Aylesworth, Thomas G. **Movie Monsters**. J.B. Lippincott, 1975.
80 p. ISBN: 0-397-31639-9; GrL: 3-6; RdL: 3
Eight chapters tell monster trivia and delectable details behind some of Hollywood's best thrillers. Among them are King King, Godzilla, The Wolf Man, The Fly (the original) and Dracula. Packed with black-and-white shots from the movies.

26.   Bare, Colleen Stanley. **To Love a Dog**. Dodd, Mead and Company, 1987.
47 p. ISBN: 0-396-09057-5; GrL: 2-4; RdL: 2
An easy text introduces different kinds of dogs and how to take care of them as pets. Accompanied by beautiful color photographs.

27. Barrett, Norman S. **Racing Cars.** Franklin Watts (Picture Library), 1984.
32 p. ISBN: 0-531-03784-3; GrL: 3-6; RdL: 4
Crisp and clear color illustrations make this slim book come alive. The author covers various classes of racing cars, including karts, rally cars, dragsters and stock and sports cars. It includes a facts-and-records section, a glossary, an index and a large diagram of the inside of a racing car.

28. Bason, Lillian. **Those Foolish Molboes.** Coward, McCann and Geoghegan, 1977.
47 p. ISBN: 0-698-20397-6 TR; 0- 698-30642-2 LB; GrL: 3-5; RdL: 3; OP
Three folktales about the silly people of Mols. These stories were written 200 years ago just for the fun of it. These are presented in a easy-to-read format.

29. Bates, Betty. **Love Is Like Peanuts.** Pocket Books, 1981.
134 p. ISBN: 0-671-47272-0 PB; GrL: 6-up; RdL: 3
Fourteen-year-old Marianne meets the challenges of caring for a mentally handicapped child but finds herself having to deal with new feelings when she falls in love with the child's older brother, Toby. Now she must confront the responsibilities of a mature relationship by learning when to say "no."

30. Bauer, Marion Dane. **On My Honor.** Clarion, 1986.
90 p. ISBN: 0-89919-439-7; GrL: 5-9; RdL: 3
Joel's best friend, Tony, drowns while they are both swimming in a dangerous river that is off limits. Since they promised their parents they wouldn't go there, Joel finds it impossible to tell the truth. Now he must deal with the painful consequences.

31. Benchley, Nathaniel. **Sam the Minuteman.** Harper & Row (I Can Read History Book), 1969.
62 p. ISBN: 0-06-020480-X LB; GrL: 1-4; RdL: 2
Sam Brown lives in Lexington, Massachusetts, when the British attack. He and his father ride to gather men to fight in the Battle of Lexington, which marked the beginning of the American Revolutionary War. Sam may be young but he fights bravely.

32. Bennett, Jay. **Dangling Witness.** Delacorte, 1974.
149 p. ISBN: 0-440-03483-3; GrL: 7-up; RdL: 2; OP
Eighteen-year-old Matt witnesses a cold-blooded murder and reluctantly decides to keep quiet after he is threatened by the killer. But he finds his promise increasingly harder to bear when he falls in love with the victim's sister.

33. Bennett, Jay. **Dark Corridor.** Franklin Watts, 1988.
151 p. ISBN: 0-531-15090-9; GrL: 9-up; RdL: 2
Kerry Lanson's girlfriend is dead, an apparent suicide after three other teens from their town have committed suicide. But Kerry is plagued by doubt and searches for the truth about her death.

34. Bennett, Jay. **Pigeon**. Methuen, 1980.
    147 p. ISBN: 0-416-30631-4; GrL: 7-up; RdL: 4; OP
    Seventeen-year-old Brian is framed for his ex-girlfriend's murder when he
    agrees to meet her one night at her apartment and finds her stabbed to death.
    As he flees the police he begins the search for the true murderer and the rea-
    son for the killing.

35. Bennett, Jay. **Say Hello to the Hit Man**. Dell, 1977.
    132 p. ISBN: 0-440-97618-9 PB; GrL: 7-up; RdL: 4; OP
    College student Fred Morgan thinks he has broken all his ties to his father's
    violent crime world until he receives a threat on his own life.

36. Bennett, Jay. **Shadows Offstage**. Thomas Nelson, Inc., 1974.
    125 p. ISBN: 0-8407-6385-9; GrL: 7-up; RdL: 2
    Peter's suspicions that his actress sister did not commit suicide grow
    stronger as he investigates, and his own life is threatened.

37. Bennett, Jay. **Skeleton Man**. Franklin Watts/Ballantine, 1986.
    170 p. ISBN: 0-531-15031-3; 0-449-70284-7 PB; GrL: 7-up; RdL: 2
    A young man is left a large amount of money by an uncle who has apparent-
    ly committed suicide. But upon further investigation he finds himself
    trapped by his uncle's murderers.

38. Berends, Polly. **Case of the Elevator Duck**. Random House, 1973.
    54 p. ISBN: 0-394-92115-1; GrL: 4-6; RdL: 3
    Gilbert is an aspiring detective who finds Easter, a lost duck, in an apart-
    ment house where pets are not allowed. So Gilbert tries to find the owner of
    the duck. He comes up with a clever solution to his problem when he is
    forced to get rid of the duck.

39. Berenstain, Stan. **Bike Lesson**. Random House (Beginner Books), 1964.
    61 p. ISBN: 0-394-80036-2; 0-394-90036-7 LB; GrL: P-3; RdL: 1
    Small bear wants to ride his new bike, but Father Bear wants even more to
    show him a few pointers. As a result, the young bear doesn't get to ride!

40. Berger, Melvin. **Photo Dictionary of Football**. Methuen, 1980.
    n.p. ISBN: 0-416-30131-2; GrL: 6-12; RdL: 5; OP
    The basics of the game are presented alphabetically from "B to U." Defines
    terms associated with high-school football in the United States and Canada.
    With black-and-white photographs.

41. Berry, James R. **Dar Tellum: Stranger from a Distant Planet**. Walker &
    Co., 1973.
    64 p. ISBN: 0-8027-6139-9; 0-8027-6140-2 PB; GrL: 4-6; RdL: 4
    Quite unexpectedly, Ralph Winston makes contact with a creature from anoth-
    er planet. They "speak" to each other silently in their minds. Dar Tellum helps
    Ralph do telekinesis, the practice of moving things by mind control. This new
    plantlike alien even helps save the Earth from impending doom.

42. Blacknall, Carolyn. **Sally Ride: America's First Woman in Space**. Dillon Press, 1984.
78 p. ISBN: 0-87518-260-7 LB; GrL: 6-9; RdL: 6
The story of the woman who became the first American female in space in 1983, from her youth to highlights of a successful NASA career. With color and black-and-white photographs.

43. Blassingame, Wyatt. **Pecos Bill Rides a Tornado**. Garrard, 1973.
30 p. ISBN: 0-8116-4038-8; GrL: 2-5; RdL: 2; OP
The famous cowboy of incredible strength and ingenuity returns in this account of how Bill lassos a tornado in order to bring back his house. In this tale, he encounters a 20-foot rattlesnake, a huge mountain lion, and rides the tornado from Oklahoma to Texas.

44. Blinn, William. **Brian's Song**. Bantam, 1972.
119 p. ISBN: 0-553-24072-2 PB; GrL: 6-up; RdL: 2
The movie script of Brian's Song tells the moving, true drama of the unusual relationship between football players Brian Piccolo and Gale Sayers. The relationship between two very different men, one white, one black, doesn't end when Brian dies of cancer.

45. Blume, Judy. **Blubber**. Bradbury Press/Dell, 1974/1986.
160 p. ISBN: 0-02-711010-9; 0-686-74492-6 PB; GrL: 4-6; RdL: 3
Jill and her friends torment an obese classmate, whom they nickname "Blubber." They force her to eat "chocolate ants," humiliate her in the girls' locker room and subject her to other sadistic experiences. But when Jill turns against the leader and sticks up for Blubber, she becomes a victim.

46. Blume, Judy. **Freckle Juice**. Four Winds/Scholastic, 1971.
40 p. ISBN: 0-590-07242-0; GrL: 2-4; RdL: 3
Andrew wants freckles, and he will go to great lengths to get them—even drinking an awful concoction called freckle juice. The "juice" is made up of grape and lemon juices, vinegar, mustard, mayonnaise, pepper, salt, ketchup, olive oil and onion. Humorous consequences follow.

47. Blume, Judy. **It's Not the End of the World**. Bradbury Press, 1972.
169 p. ISBN: 0-87888-042-9; GrL: 5-8; RdL: 3
Karen's family life as she knows it is ending even as she fights hard to keep her separating parents together. She comes to the realization that she cannot keep the inevitable from happening and learns to cope.

48. Blume, Judy. **Tales of a Fourth Grade Nothing**. E.P. Dutton/Dell, 1972/1981.
128 p. ISBN: 0-525-40720-0 LB; 0-440-48474-X PB; GrL: 3-6; RdL: 3
Hilarious plot unfolds as Peter shares the dastardly escapades of his two-and-a-half-year-old brother, Fudge, who never provides a dull moment. Among other things, he plasters green stamps all over his father's boss's suitcase, nearly ruins a TV commercial and carries on in the most unusual places and ways.

49. Blume, Judy. **Tiger Eyes**. Bradbury Press, 1981.
    206 p. ISBN: 0-87888-185-9; GrL: 6-up; RdL: 3
    Resettled in a new town, Davey with her family recovers from the shocking
    murder of her father. She comes to grip with new adjustments and feelings
    even though her new home out West is radically different from the East
    Coast home she left.

50. Bonham, Frank. **Durango Street**. Dell, 1965.
    187 p. ISBN: 0-440-92183-X; GrL: 8-up; RdL: 6
    Rufus Henry is just out of a detention home when he violates parole by join-
    ing a local gang in an attempt to clean up the Projects. But he finds himself
    getting more involved with the violence he sought to avoid.

51. Boutis, Victoria. **Katy Did It**. Greenwillow, 1982.
    88 p. ISBN: 0-688-00688-4; 0-688-00689-2 LB; GrL: 4-6; RdL: 3; OP
    Eight-year-old Katy decides to go hiking and camping overnight in the
    mountains with her father and their dog. She is enthusiastic about going.
    However, the actual experience is, at first, less than desirable and, at times,
    frightening. Their trip teaches her a lot about life and its transitory nature.

52. Branley, Franklyn Mansfield. **Eclipse: Darkness in Daytime**. Harper &
    Row (Let's-Read-And-Find-Out-Science Book), 1988 rev.ed.
    32 p. ISBN: 0-690-04617-0 TR; 0-690-04619-7 LB; GrL: 1-4; RdL: 2
    An easily explained occurrence that has intrigued people for centuries. The
    causes of a solar eclipse, as well as ancient beliefs, are presented. Directions
    for making a sun projection are given for safe "viewing" of an eclipse.

53. Broekel, Ray. **Football**. Childrens Press (New True Books), 1982.
    45 p. ISBN: 0-516-01629-6 LB;0-516-41629-4 PB; GrL: 3-6; RdL: 2
    The game of football is simply explained in large print with color pho-
    tographs, a glossary and an index. Discusses high-school, college and pro-
    fessional games, mentioning famous teams from the National League.

54. Bromley, Dudley. **Balloon Spies**. Pitman Learning Inc., 1981.
    75 p. ISBN: 0-8224-6730-5 PB; GrL: 7-up; RdL: 4
    Hot-air balloonists Lillian and Oren go undercover to help the Union army
    fight the Confederates by spying from their balloon. Historical facts are
    interspersed with the story throughout the book.

55. Brown, Drollene P. **Sybil Rides for Independence**. Albert Whitman & Co.,
    1985.
    48 p. ISBN: 0-8075-7684-0; GrL: 4-6; RdL: 4
    True account of 16-year-old Sybil Ludington's dangerou ride through the
    night to warn the Minutemen of the British attack on Danbury, Connecticut,
    in 1777. Containing six chapters, the final one tells more about the Ameri-
    can Revolution, putting this episode into perspective.

56. Brown, Fern G. **Teen Guide to Childbirth**. Franklin Watts, 1988.
    62 p. ISBN: 0-531-10573-3; GrL: 6-up; RdL: 4
    A practical look at birth with its preparations, signs of labor, types of birthing methods, stages of labor and what to do after the child is born. Part of the Teen Guides Series, this includes a glossary and index.

57. Bulla, Clyde Robert. **Chalk Box Kid**. Random House (Stepping Stone Books), 1987.
    56 p. ISBN: 0-394-99102-8 LB; GrL: 2-4; RdL: 2
    A nine-year-old boy lives in a house with no room for a garden, so he creates an imaginative and striking garden of his own in a unusual places using unusual materials.

58. Bulla, Clyde Robert. **My Friend the Monster**. Thomas Y. Crowell, 1980.
    96 p. ISBN: 0-690-04031-8; 0-690-04032-6 LB; GrL: 2-5; RdL: 1
    A young prince is held captive by his wicked parents until one day he befriends a monster who lives in a hill.

59. Bulla, Clyde Robert. **Pirate's Promise**. Harper & Row, 1958.
    87 p. ISBN: 0-690-62656-8; GrL: 3-6; RdL: 2; OP
    Tom Pippin and his sister, Dinah, are orphans who are separated by their malicious uncle. Tom is bonded to the captain of a ship for seven years while his sister remains in England. Tom's adventure begins when pirates capture the ship and force the crew to abandon it.

60. Bunting, Eve. **Ghosts of Departure Point**. J.B. Lippincott/Scholastic, 1982.
    113 p. ISBN: 0-397-31998-3 LB; 0-590-33116-7 PB; GrL: 5-up; RdL: 2
    Two victims of car crashes over a deadly cliff meet, fall in love and discover a way to redeem their selfish acts that caused their cars to wreck, killing all occupants.

61. Bunting, Eve. **Girl in the Painting**. Pitman (Fastback Romance), 1984.
    37 p. ISBN: 0-8224-3528-4 PB; GrL: 6-up; RdL: 5
    Carla Birch, a new girl at school, is auctioned off to help raise money for the girls' sport's program. It's supposed to be an honor, but she's been set up by the cute and popular Troy Lester, who bids on her as a joke — that is, until Troy realizes that he really is interested in her as a person and an artist.

62. Bunting, Eve. **How Many Days to America? A Thanksgiving Story**. Clarion, 1988.
    32 p. ISBN: 0-89919-521-0; GrL: 1-4; RdL: 2
    A small fishing boat filled with refugees battles the elements and bandits as they sail the Caribbean and head for America. Surprisingly, they land on Thanksgiving Day, giving a contemporary meaning to this traditional holiday.

63. Bunting, Eve. **If I Asked You, Would You Stay?** J.B. Lippincott, 1984.
151 p. ISBN: 0-397-32065-5 TR;0-397-32066-3 LB; GrL: 7-up; RdL: 3
Seventeen-year-old Crow is a loner and lives in a secret apartment on the boardwalk. His loner existence is threatened when he rescues a girl who's tried to commit suicide in the ocean one night. Despite his resentment upon having to share his hideaway, he finds himself falling in love with her.

64. Bunting, Eve. **Is Anybody There?** J.B. Lippincott, 1988.
170 p. ISBN: 0-397-32303-4 LB; GrL: 4-8; RdL: 3
After discovering that several household items have disappeared, Marcus, a latchkey child, suspects that someone may be prowling inside his house while he is at school.

65. Bunting, Eve. **Janet Hamm Needs a Date for the Dance.**Clarion, 1986.
104 p. ISBN: 0-89919-408-7; GrL: 6-9; RdL: 3
This is a companion book to Karen Kepplewhite Is the World's Best Kisser. This time it's Janet who tries to find the perfect boy to ask to a seventh grade dance. It gets complicated when she innocently goes along with a lie that she's going with her older brother's friend.

66. Bunting, Eve. **Karen Kepplewhite Is the World's Best Kisser**. Pocket Books/Clarion, 1983/1984.
87 p. ISBN: 0-89919-182-7; 0-671-52734-7 PB; GrL: 4-6; RdL: 2
Karen and her best friend, Janet, inexperienced in the ways of love, consult a book on the art of kissing to prepare for an upcoming boy/girl birthday party. Despite all of their anxiety, they learn that there's more to life and love than doing things by the book.

67. Bunting, Eve. **Skate Patrol**. Albert Whitman & Co., 1980.
40 p. ISBN: 0-8075-7393-0; GrL: 2-4; RdL: 2
In this first of the series, two boys skate and sleuth through the park near their apartment complex. They observe a very suspicious man and believe him to be the Creep Thief, who robs senior citizens. The plot takes off through lively dialogue and short chapters. Illustrations compliment the text.

68. Bunting, Eve. **Skateboard Four**. Albert Whitman & Co., 1976.
63 p. ISBN: 0-8075-7392-2; GrL: 4-7; RdL: 3; OP
Morgan, the leader of a skateboard club, has to decide whether to let in a new member. Morgan feels threatened by the new guy because he can perform better maneuvers on his board. Morgan comes up with the ultimate test to challenge the new guy. In the end, he shows that leaders must make responsible decisions.

69. Bunting, Eve. **Someone Is Hiding on Alcatraz Island.** Houghton Mifflin Company, 1984.
    136 p. ISBN: 0-89919-219-X; GrL: 6-up; RdL: 3
    Fourteen-year-old Danny riles a local gang when he intervenes to help a woman during a mugging. Now the Outlaws are out for him even as he flees to hide on Alcatraz Island.

70. Burchard, Marshall. **Terry Bradshaw.** Putnam (Sports Hero), 1980.
    94 p. ISBN: 0-399-61133-9; GrL: 3-6; RdL: 4; OP
    One in a series of 20 or so biographies of famous sports stars. There are nine chapters that contain very large type and much leading. Black-and-white photographs from Bradshaw's quarterbacking career are highlighted. There are some difficult words, but these are football terms.

71. Butterworth, W.E. **LeRoy and the Old Man.** Scholastic (Vagabond Books), 1980.
    168 p. ISBN: 0-590-32635-X PB; GrL: 7-up; RdL: 3
    LeRoy witnesses a stabbing and is called to testify against members of the Wolves gang. Fearing for his own life he flees to New Orleans to live with his estranged grandfather, a man he hardly knows but who teaches him the meaning of self-respect.

72. Byars, Betsy. **Beans on the Roof.** Delacorte, 1988.
    65 p. ISBN: 0-440-50055-9; GrL: 2-4; RdL: 2
    Each of the members of the Bean family tries to write a poem inspired by the roof of their apartment and what they see from it. As they create, they realize how glad they are to be a family together.

73. Byars, Betsy. **Burning Questions of Bingo Brown.** Viking, Kestrel, 1988.
    166 p. ISBN: 0-670-81932-8; GrL: 5-up; RdL: 5
    Bingo is keeping a notebook filled with things that confuse and worry especially his growing romantic urges and his concerns about his troubled teacher's attempted suicide. Writing both his funny and serious thoughts help him cope with the changing world around him.

74. Byars, Betsy. **Golly Sisters Go West.** Harper & Row (I Can Read), 1985.
    64 p. ISBN: 0-06-020884-8 LB; GrL: K-3; RdL: 1
    Two zany sisters, May-May and Rose, head west in their covered wagon, sharing mirth along the way. They put on singing and dancing shows, laughing along their way.

75. Byars, Betsy. **Good-bye, Chicken Little.** Harper & Row, 1979.
    101 p. ISBN: 0-06-020907-0; 0-06-020911-9 LB; GrL: 4-6; RdL: 4
    Moving, emotional account of a young boy who could not prevent the death of his daredevil uncle. Jimmy learns to come to grips with his guilt, his eccentric family and, most important, comes to love his relatives for who they are.

76. Byars, Betsy. **Summer of the Swans**. Puffin, 1984.
    142 p. ISBN: 0-670-68190-3; 0-14-031420-2 PB; GrL: 6-9; RdL: 6
    Sara's younger, mentally handicapped brother disappears one day. As she
    searches for him she learns the importance of caring for someone else and in
    doing so learns more about herself.

77. Cameron, Ann. **Julian's Glorious Summer**. Random House (Stepping
    Stone Books), 1987.
    62 p. ISBN: 0-394-89117-1 TR; 0-394-99117-6 LB; GrL: 1-3; RdL: 2
    When his best friend, Gloria, receives a new bicycle, Julian spends his sum-
    mer days avoiding her because of his fear of riding bicycles. Until one day
    his father buys him a bike of his own and then he must face his fears.

78. Cameron, Ann. **Julian, Secret Agent**. Random House (Stepping Stone
    Books), 1988.
    63 p. ISBN: 0-394-81949-7 PB; 0-394-91949-1 LB; GrL: 1-3; RdL: 2
    Julian, his brother Huey and friend Gloria become "crimebusters" rescue a
    dog trapped in a hot car, and keep a toddler from drowning, and decide to go
    after a real bank robber.

79. Cameron, Ann. **More Stories Julian Tells**. Alfred A. Knopf, 1986.
    82 p. ISBN: 0-394-86969-9; 0-394-96969-3 LB; GrL: 2-4; RdL: 3
    In this sequel to The Stories Julian Tells the tales of imagination and warmth
    continue with episodes of secret messages in bottles and a bet with a friend
    who claims she can move the sun.

80. Cameron, Ann. **Stories Julian Tells**. Random House, 1981.
    71 p. ISBN: 0-394-84301-0; 0-394-94301-5 LB; GrL: 2-4; RdL: 3
    A collection of humorous tales surrounding a young black boy and his fam-
    ily and friends. Stories include making wishes on the tail of a kite and the
    discovery of mysterious catalog cats who grow gardens. Sequel is More Sto-
    ries Julian Tells.

81. Carlson, Natalie Savage. **Ghost in the Lagoon**. Lothrop, Lee & Shepard,
    1984.
    40 p. ISBN: 0-688-03794-1; 0-688-03795-X LB; GrL: 2-4; RdL: 2; OP
    Timmy Hawkins lives with his poor family in a tumbledown shack. One
    night he and his father go catfishing in the lagoon, which people claim is
    haunted. Sure enough, they come face-to-face with a sinister pirate ghost
    who guards his buried treasure. Timmy finds a way to outwit this spectre.

82. Cavanna, Betty. **Banner Year**. Morrow, 1987.
    217 p. ISBN: 0-688-05779-9; GrL: 7-up; RdL: 4
    Cindy, a sophomore, cares only about horses despite the growing affections
    of a new boy, Tad. When her favorite horse, Banner, is wounded, she leads
    an all-encompassing campaign to save his life. Tad feels rejected but soon
    learns to appreciate her dedication as they experience a budding rommance.

83. Chaikin, Miriam. **Aviva's Piano**. Clarion, 1986.
43 p. ISBN: 0-89919-367-6; GrL: 3-4; RdL: 3
Aviva has moved from Argentina to an Israeli kibbutz and one of her prized possessions is her piano. But it is too large to fit through the door of her home. A terrorist's bomb hits her house; fortunately, the only damage is that there is now a hole big enough in which to insert the piano.

84. Chew, Ruth. **Do-It-Yourself Magic**. Hastings House, 1987.
127 p. ISBN: 0-8038-9299-3; GrL: 2-5; RdL: 3
Rachel and Scott buy a Build-Anything Kit that is really magic. With it they can build whatever they want, change themselves, and go back in time. Scott shrinks down to drive a stock car racer and travels back to the days of knights and castles.

85. Chew, Ruth. **No Such Thing as a Witch**. Hastings House, 1980.
112 p. ISBN: 0-8038-5073-5; GrL: 4-6; RdL: 2
Nora and Tad have an eccentric neighbor ... she's a witch! The story takes off once the children find out that the wonderful fudge that Maggie (the witch) makes is enchanted. One piece makes them appreciate animals, two pieces make them able to communicate with animals, but three turn them into animals.

86. Christian, Mary Blount. **Mysterious Case Case**. E.P. Dutton (Determined Detectives), 1985.
48 p. ISBN: 0-525-44217-0; GrL: 3-5; RdL: 4
This action-packed caper takes off when Fenton P. Smith and his friend, Gerald Grubbs, find out that the briefcase Fenton has picked up contains a million dollars. He inadvertently bumped into a man who had a case similar to his, and the switch was accidently made.

87. Christopher, Matt. **Hit-Away Kid**. Little, Brown and Company, 1988.
60 p. ISBN: 0-316-13995-5; GrL: 3-5; RdL: 3
Barry McGee, the hit-away batter for the Peach Street Mudders, cares only about winning to the extreme, and he will do anything to do so, including bending the rules. But when the pitcher of a team they're playing pulls some questionable moves, Barry gains a new perspective on sportsmanship.

88. Christopher, Matt. **Red-Hot Hightops**. Little, Brown and Company, 1987.
148 p. ISBN: 0-316-14056-2; GrL: 6-9; RdL: 3
Kelly Roberts is usually afraid to play basketball in front of other people even though she's on the school team. One day she receives a pair of red sneakers as an anonymous gift. Suddenly she's confident and aggressive on the court. She must discover whether the shoes are magic of the power lies in herself.

89. Christopher, Matt. **Tackle without a Team**. Little, Brown and Company, 1989.
    145 p. ISBN: 0-316-14067-8; GrL: 6-9; RdL: 2
    Scott is unjustly dismissed from the football team when marijuana is discovered in his bag. Now he must find out who planted it there so he can rejoin the team and clear himself with his parents.

90. Clark, Margaret Goff. **Barney and the UFO**. Dodd, Mead and Company, 1979.
    159 p. ISBN: 0-396-07711-0; GrL: 4-7; RdL: 4; OP
    Barney, a foster child, meets Tibbo, an alien from the planet Ornam who is lonely and wants to take Barney home with him.

91. Claypool, Jane. **Jasmine Finds Love**. Westminister Press, 1982.
    80 p. ISBN: 0-664-32699-4; GrL: 6-up; RdL: 3
    Jasmine lives with a strict father who forbids her to date. He changes his mind when a distant cousin arrives. But Jasmine is torn between her emotions because this boy isn't as attractive as Jasmine's first love, whom she has been forbidden to see. She learns that romance can grow between good friends.

92. Cleary, Beverly. **Dear Mr. Henshaw**. Morrow, 1983.
    133 p. ISBN: 0-688-02406-8 LB; GrL: 5-8; RdL: 5
    Leigh's parents have divorced, he attends a new school and the only way he can cope is by writing letters to his favorite childhood author. It becomes a special form of therapy when he doesn't send most of the letters but keeps a journal of his feelings instead.

93. Cleary, Beverly. **Socks**. Morrow, 1973.
    155 p. ISBN: 0-688-20067-2; 0-688-30067-7 LB; GrL: 4-6; RdL: 2
    The hilarious episodes of Socks, the pampered cat of the Brickers household, are told in this story. He doesn't like rivals to his attention and mayhem results when the Brickers have a new "pet," a baby.

94. Clifford, Eth. **Harvey's Marvelous Monkey Mystery**. Houghton Mifflin Company, 1987.
    119 p. ISBN: 0-395-42622-7; GrL: 4-6; RdL: 4
    Harvey Wilson finds himself caught in a peculiar mystery when a monkey shows up in his bedroom window in the middle of the night. He and his visiting "weird" cousin, Nora, pool their talents to find out why the monkey's appeared.

95. Clifford, Eth. **Help! I'm a Prisoner in the Library**. Houghton Mifflin Company, 1979.
    103 p. ISBN: 0-395-28478-3; 0-590-33481-6 PB; GrL: 4-6; RdL: 2
    Mary-Rose and Jo-Beth get an unexpected surprise when they become trapped in the library during a blizzard. Their father's car runs out of gas, and when he leaves for a gas station they trek to a curious old library. They spend an eerie night in this old place filled with wooden dolls and animals.

96. Clifford, Eth. **I Never Wanted to Be Famous**. Houghton Mifflin Company, 1986.
131 p. ISBN: 0-395-40420-7; GrL: 4-6; RdL: 4
Goodwin "Goody" Drake Tribble becomes an instant local hero when he saves a boy from choking while at the dentist. Before this fame dies out, he finds himself catching a fellow student as she accidently falls from a ladder. With all this publicity he may even become president of the United States!

97. Cluck, Bob. **Baserunning**. Contemporary Books (The Winning Edge Series), 1987.
90 p. ISBN: 0-8092-4784-4 PB; GrL: 6-9; RdL: 6
Tips on how to improve baserunning are included in this book. Others in the series are Shortstop and Hitting.

98. Cluck, Bob. **Hitting**. Contemporary Books (The Winning Edge Series), 1987.
79 p. ISBN: 0-8092-4786-0 PB; GrL: 6-9; RdL: 6
Cluck tells how to improve baseball techniques including batting swing, hitting the ball, solving other hitting problems and practice tips. With photographs and index. Others in the series: Baserunning and Shortstop.

99. Cluck, Bob. **Shortstop**. Contemporary Books (The Winning Edge Series), 1987.
91 p. ISBN: 0-8092-4785-2 PB; GrL: 6-9; RdL: 6
Tips on improving the shortstop position on the baseball field. Others in the series: Hitting and Baserunning.

100. Cohen, Daniel. **Headless Roommate and Other Tales of Terror**. Bantam, 1980.
138 p. ISBN: 0-553-20382-7 PB; GrL: 7-up; RdL: 5
Nineteen horrifying stories based on real legends and folklore with modern, urban settings. For example, a murder on a college campus or the story of the used car with the mysteriously foul odor.

101. Cohen, Daniel. **Monsters of Star Trek**. Archway, 1980.
117 p. ISBN: 0-671-56057-3; GrL: 7-up; RdL: 7
Alien creatures from the popular television show, "Star Trek," are featured by type. For example, "Mind Benders," "Alien Races," "Androids," etc. Accompanied by black-and-white photos from the show and an index.

102. Cohen, Daniel. **Restless Dead**. Archway, 1984.
103 p. ISBN: 0-671-64373 PB; GrL: 4-up; RdL: 4
This features ghostly stories from around the world including: "The Ghost of the Murdered Mummy," "Stolen Liver" and nine other chilling tales.

103. Cole, Brock. **Goats**. Farrar, Straus & Giroux, 1987.
     183 p. ISBN: 0-374-32678-9; GrL: 6-up; RdL: 2
     Howie and Laura, victims of a cruel prank, are left stranded and naked on an island during summer camp. It is a story of their courage and strength when they decide never to return to camp. They grow close as friends despite their humiliating experience.

104. Cole, Joanna. **Asking about Sex and Growing Up**. Morrow Jr., 1988.
     90 p. ISBN: 0-688-06927-4; 0-688-06928-2 PB; GrL: 5-up; RdL: Varies
     A question-and-answer book for pre-adolescent and teenage boys and girls. Topics addressed include crushes, physical differences of boys and girls, sexual intercourse, birth and birth control, homosexuality and AIDS.

105. Cole, Joanna. **My Puppy Is Born**. Morrow, 1973.
     n.p. ISBN: 0-688-20078-8; 0-688-30078-2 LB; GrL: 1-4; RdL: 2; OP
     A young girl tells how a puppy is born and the subsequent first eight weeks of his life until she takes him home with her. Accompanied by graphic but warm black-and-white photographs.

106. Cole, Joanna. **Missing Tooth**. Random House (Step Into Reading), 1988.
     48 p. ISBN: 0-394-89279-8 PB; 0-394-99279-2 LB; GrL: 1-3; RdL: 1
     Two friends, Arlo and Robby, are alike in many ways: they have the same kinds of pets, they both love the same foods, and they even have the same tooth missing. When Robby loses one more tooth than Arlo their friendship is threatened.

107. Colver, Anne. **Abraham Lincoln**. Dell, 1960.
     76 p. ISBN: 0-440-40001-5; GrL: 4-6; RdL: 2
     Beginner's account of the life of Lincoln from his early childhood through assassination. His love of reading, cleverness, and even mischievousness are pointed out. The story has plenty of dialogue and is interesting to read.

108. Conford, Ellen. **And This Is Laura**. Little, Brown and Company, 1977.
     179 p. ISBN: 0-316-15300-1; GrL: 4-7; RdL: 4
     Laura feels she is an outcast in a family of achievers until she discovers she is a psychic and can look into the future. She also learns that this can be a curse as well as a gift.

109. Conford, Ellen. **Case for Jenny Archer**. Little, Brown and Company (Springboard), 1988.
     61 p. ISBN: 0-316-15266-8; GrL: 2-4; RdL: 3
     A companion book to A Job For Jenny Archer. In this story, Jenny is bored over summer vacation so she reads three mystery stories in a row. After, she is convinced that she smells trouble across the street. She suspects they are up to no good and decides to investigate for herself.

110. Conford, Ellen. **If This Is Love, I'll Take Spaghetti**. Four Winds, 1983.
165 p. ISBN: 0-02-724250-1; GrL: 6-up; RdL: 4
The problems, joys and anxieties of teenage crushes and first loves are humorously presented in these nine stories. Whether it's going on an intense diet to become more attractive or two close friends unknowingly sharing the same guy, fun abounds.

111. Conford, Ellen. **Job for Jenny Archer**. Little, Brown and Company, 1988.
76 p. ISBN: 0-316-15262-5; GrL: 2-4; RdL: 3
Jenny's family has money troubles; she is convinced that they are poor because her parents refuse to buy her a horse or a swimming pool. So she comes up with her own plans to make money, including one idea that puts her own house up for sale. Companion book to A Case for Jenny Archer.

112. Conford, Ellen. **Strictly for Laughs**. Pacer Books (Putnam), 1985.
155 p. ISBN: 0-448-47754-8; GrL: 6-up; RdL: 4
Joey Merino lives to make people laugh, but she finds that all she really wants is to be taken seriously—by Peter, an aspiring disc jockey. She tries to convince him that she isn't kidding about their relationship.

113. Conford, Ellen. **Things I Did for Love**. Bantam, 1987.
137 p. ISBN: 0-553-05431-7; GrL: 6-up; RdL: 4
Stephanie chooses the topic of love for her research project in psychology class, hoping that she can gain some personal experience in an area in which she is sadly lacking expertise. As a result she draws some surprising conclusions about herself, boys and romance.

114. Corbett, Scott. **Great McGoniggle Rides Shotgun**. Little, Brown and Company, 1977.
52 p. ISBN: 0-316-15729-5; 0-440-43313-4 PB; GrL: 3-6; RdL: 2; OP
Mac McGoniggle and his friend, Ken, accept a ride with a nervous stranger and find themselves involved in a robbery. Others in the series: The Great McGoniggle Switches Pitches (1980), The Great McGoniggle's Gray Ghost (1975) and The Great McGoniggle's Key Play (1976).

115. Cowen, Eve. **Catch the Sun**. Fearon (SporTellers), 1981.
60 p. ISBN: 0-8224-6475-6 PB; GrL: 9-up; RdL: 5
Deena LaSalle, an architect, gets a big account to design a major New York City bank at the same time that she needs to train for the NYC marathon. Her boss and some of her colleagues want her to quit the running or risk the account, but Deena is determined to success at both.

116. Cowen, Eve. **High Escape**. Fearon (SporTellers), 1981.
60 p. ISBN: 0-8224-6478-0 PB; GrL: 9-up; RdL: 4
Dory Lane, a member of the U.S. Alpine Ski Team, undergoes the fierce competition of racing the champion Irina Kapov in an exciting downhill race.

117. Curtis, Philip. **Invasion of the Brain Sharpeners**. Alfred A. Knopf (Capers), 1981.
117 p. ISBN: 0-394-94676-6; 0-394-84676-1 PB; GrL: 4-6; RdL: 3
Michael is the only one who outsmarts the Brain Sharpeners, who have captured the minds of his teacher and his classmates. The aliens brainwash their victims into studying harder so the aliens can colonize one of their planets with the young people from Earth. A fast-paced, lighthearted thriller.

118. Cynthia, Blair. **Marshmallow Masquerade**. Ballantine, 1987.
136 p. ISBN: 0-449-70217-0 PB; GrL: 6-up; RdL: 4
The twins, Susan and Christine Pratt, of The Pumpkin Principle and The Hot Fudge Sunday Affair are back. Here they find a foolproof way to find out what makes boys tick when Chris dresses herself as a boy to learn first-hand information.

119. Danziger, Paula. **Cat Ate My Gymsuit**. Alfred A. Knopf/Dell (paper), 1974.
119 p. ISBN: 0-440-91612-7; 0-440-41612-4 PB; GrL: 6-9; RdL: 5
A ninth-grader learns that working things out is part of growing up when her favorite teacher is suspended and the students rally to her side. Marcy also comes to terms with her abusive father.

120. Danziger, Paula. **Remember Me to Harold Square**. Dell, 1987.
139 p. ISBN: 0-440-20153-5 PB; GrL: 6-up; RdL: 2
Kendra Kaye, her brother "O.K.," and a visiting friend, Frank, join together in the summer fun of a Serendipity Scavenger Hunt through New York City. Designed by their parents to keep them out of trouble as well as provide fun, the hunt takes them to museums and eateries discovering a city they thought they knew.

121. Davidson, Margaret. **Story of Benjamin Franklin, Amazing American**. Dell, 1988.
92 p. ISBN: 0-440-40021-X; GrL: 4-6; RdL: 3
The story of Benjamin Franklin: printer, inventor, statesman, writer, and more. This tells of his resourcefulness and his many talents. Highlights of his exciting life are listed at the end of the book.

122. Davis, Jenny. **Sex Education**. Orchard (Watts), 1988.
150 p. ISBN: 0-531-08356-X LB; 0-531-05756-9; GrL: 7-9; RdL: 2
Livvie Sinclair and David Kindler team up for an assignment for their sex education class. Together they care for a troubled, young, pregnant neighbor and in doing so learn the true meaning of love and pain.

123. De Leeuw, Adele. **Paul Bunyan Finds a Wife**. Garrard, 1969.
30 p. ISBN: 0-8116-4013-2; GrL: 2-5; RdL: 2; OP
The legend of Paul Bunyan continues in this simple account of how Paul meets Carrie, his pancake-flipping wife. His Blue Ox reappears to help him and his logger pals fell the forests of Wisconsin. Unusual but humorous solutions to problems abound in this tall tale.

124. DeClements, Barthe. **Nothing's Fair in Fifth Grade**. Viking, 1981.
137 p. ISBN: 0-670-51741-0; GrL: 4-6; RdL: 3
Jenny wants to befriend a new girl in her class who is overweight and steals money. The other classmates are cruel to the student, so Jenny risks her own popularity when she attempts to understand the new girl, Elsie.

125. Delton, Judy. **Only Jody**. Houghton Mifflin Company, 1982.
95 p. ISBN: 0-395-32080-1; GrL: 4-6; RdL: 3
The amusing story tells of the only boy in a household of three women (a boy with a girl's name, to boot). His mother enrolls him in parochial school, much to his dismay, as this is the eighth school he's been to in ten years. But he teams up with Otto and his wild ideas, such as looking for drug pushers.

126. DePaola, Tomie. **Quicksand Book**. Holiday House, 1977.
n.p. ISBN: 0-8234-0291-6; GrL: K-3; RdL: 2
An amusing way to learn about this natural phenomenon that is simply explained by Jungle boy after Jungle girl falls into it. Jungle boy explains rescue techniques as she sinks. Finally, he saves her only to fall in himself.

127. Devaney, John. **Secrets of the Super Athletes: Soccer**. Dell, 1982.
128 p. ISBN: 0-440-98399-1 PB; GrL: 6-up; RdL: 6; OP
Tips from soccer professionals include handling the ball, footwork, exercises and even inside secrets. Black-and-white photos of uneven quality accompany the text. A special quiz is included in the back so the reader can test his or her skills. Others in series: Football, Basketball and Baseball.

128. DeWeese, Gene. **Nightmares from Space**. Franklin Watts, 1981.
88 p. ISBN: 0-531-04338-x; GrL: 6-12; RdL: 2; OP
Four teenagers encounter an alien force from another planet that leaves them with extrasensory abilities which can be used to do good. But for Steve, this newly acquired power is a dangerous one.

129. Dickmeyer, Lowell A. **Soccer Is for Me**. Lerner Publications Company, 1978.
47 p. ISBN: 0-8225-1076-7; GrL: 2-4; RdL: 2; OP
This is one in a series of over 45 sports books told from a child's point of view. It gives very simple explanations of how the sport is played and what it feels like to play (and win or lose), with some technique. There is a section at the end explaining key terminology used in the sport.

130. Dolan, Edward F. **Great Moments in the Super Bowl**. Franklin Watts, 1982.
90 p. ISBN: 0-531-04408-4; GrL: 4-8; RdL: 3; OP
Accounts of the first 15 Super Bowl games from 1967 to 1981. Highlights key plays and players; includes black-and-white photographs and an index.

131. Dolan, Edward F. **Great Mysteries of the Air**. Dodd, Mead and Company, 1983.
     127 p. ISBN: 0-396-08185-1; GrL: 4-6; RdL: 4
     This book provides exciting accounts of several puzzling occurrences involving air travel. Included are episodes from World War II to the early 1980s. Some involve benevolent ghosts, others unusual disappearances, such as those of Amelia Earhart and the victims of the Bermuda Triangle.

132. Donnelly, Judy. **Titanic Lost and Found**. Random House (Step Into Reading), 1987.
     48 p. ISBN: 0-394-88669-0 TR; 0-394-98669-5 LB; GrL: 2-4; RdL: 2
     An easy-to-read look at the sinking of the famous ship, the Titanic, and the discovery of the remains and its treasures. With color sketches.

133. Donnelly, Judy. **True-Life Treasure Hunts**. Random House, 1984.
     68 p. ISBN: 0-394-86801-3; 0-394-96801-8 LB; GrL: 4-6; RdL: 4
     This nonfiction account of the quest for lost treasure includes the discoveries of the sunken city of Port Royal, a shipwreck off the coast of Florida, King Tut's tomb, and the Sacred Well of Chichen Itza, Mexico. There are five sections telling tales of outlaws and pirates.

134. Donnelly, Judy. **Tut's Mummy: Lost...and Found**. Random House (Step Into Reading), 1988.
     48 p. ISBN: 0-394-89189-9 PB; 0-394-99189-3 LB; GrL: 3-4; RdL: 2
     A fascinating look at the discovery of Tutankhamen's tomb by Howard Carter. Shares the methods used for excavating the treasure and the actual tomb. With color and black-and-white photographs and illustrations.

135. Donnelly, Judy. **Who Shot the President? The Death of John F. Kennedy**. Random House (Step Into Reading), 1988.
     48 p. ISBN: 0-394-99944-4 LB; 0-394-89944-X PB; GrL: 3-6; RdL: 4
     Informative account of the events of the day President Kennedy was assassinated in Dallas, Texas. It explores many of the unanswered questions surrounding the case including the possibility of conspiracy and the reports of the Warren Commission. With color and black-and-white photographs.

136. Dubowski, Cathy East. **Pretty Good Magic**. Random House (Step Into Reading), 1988.
     48 p. ISBN: 0-394-89068-X TR; 0-394-99068-4 LB; GrL: 1-3; RdL: 2
     Presto, a magician, tries to impress the town of Forty Winks with a super-spectacular trick that backfires and produces more rabbits than he can handle.

137. Duncan, Lois. **I Know What You Did Last Summer**. Simon & Schuster, 1973.
     198 p. ISBN: 0-671-63970-6 PB; GrL: 7-up; RdL: 3
     Four teenagers make a secret pact after they accidently kill a boy with their speeding car. Six months go by without suspicion until someone seeks to ruin them in revenge.

138. DuPrau, Jeanne. **Golden God**. Fearon (TaleSpinners I), 1981.
76 p. ISBN: 0-8224-6727-5 PB; GrL: 9-up; RdL: 5
Three members of an archeological dig discover a solid-gold statue of Kalim while searching for an ancient city. As Val, Bruce and Dr. Selk carry the treasure through the burning desert, misfortunes befall them and they wonder if the statue is cursed.

139. Edwards, Anne. **Great Houdini**. Putnam, 1977.
62 p. ISBN: 0-399-20530-6; 0-399-61020-0 LB; GrL: 4-6; RdL: 3; OP
This book records the life of Ehrich Weiss, better known as Houdini, from boyhood to death, with an emphasis on his physical strength and determination. This poor boy found ingenious ways to raise money for his family. He was intrigued with magic and performed his own acts.

140. Eichhorn, Dennis P. **Springsteen**. Turman Publishing Company, 1986.
75 p. ISBN: 0-89872-204-7 PB; GrL: 6-up; RdL: 4
One of the Reading Success paperbacks on contemporary rock stars, this one features the life of a rock sensation from his childhood in New Jersey to his climb up the rock music charts. Black-and-white photographs enhance the informative text. Like the others in this series, a glossary of terms appears after each chapter.

141. Eisenberg, Lisa. **Killer Music**. Fearon (Laura Brewster Book), 1980.
60 p. ISBN: 0-8224-1085-0 PB; GrL: 6-up; RdL: 2
Laura, an insurance investigator, and her parrot travel to England where she solves the mystery of a murdered rock musician. Others in the series are: House of Laughs, Tiger Rose, Fast-Food King, Falling Star and Golden Idol.

142. Eisenberg, Lisa, and Katy Hall. **101 Ghost Jokes**. Scholastic, 1988.
94 p. ISBN: 0-590-41811-4 PB; GrL: 4-up; RdL: 2
Puns and silliness abound in this collection of spooky riddles.

143. Eisler, Colin. **Cats Know Best**. Dial, 1988.
n.p. ISBN: 0-8037-0503-4; 0-8037-0560-3 LB; GrL: P-3; RdL: 1
A vibrant, unscientific but playful look at the nature of cats. Filled with wonderful illustrations and a simple text.

144. Epstein, Sam, and Beryl Epstein. **Harriet Tubman: Guide to Freedom**. Garrard, 1968.
96 p. ISBN: 0-8116-4550-9; GrL: 4-6; RdL: 2; OP
Inspiring account of the life of black Underground Railroad heroine. Highlights her rise from slavery to lecturer to her death at the age of 90. Easy-to-read, yet poignant and informative. One in a series, Americans All, featuring real people who have attained personal success in spite of adversity.

145. Etrat, Jonathan. **Aliens for Breakfast**. Random House (Stepping Stone Books), 1988.
62 p. ISBN: 0-394-82093-2 PB;0-394-92093-7 LB; GrL: 3-4; RdL: 3
An alien is freeze-dried in a cereal box and beamed to Earth to stop an enemy takeover of the planet. "Aric" and Richard team up to fight the enemy, who has disguised himself as the new, cool kid in the class.

146. Eyerly, Jeannette. **Someone to Love Me**. J.B. Lippincott, 1987.
168 p. ISBN: 0-397-32205-4;0-397-32206-2 LB; GrL: 7-up; RdL: 3
Fifteen-year-old Patrice wanted to feel needed and wanted, but she finds herself pregnant and she decides to keep the baby.

147. Fife, Dale. **Follow That Ghost**. E.P. Dutton, 1979.
58 p. ISBN: 0-525-30010-4; GrL: 2-4; RdL: 2; OP
Simple tale of two amateur sleuths who try to discover who has been causing mysterious sounds at night in a young girl's apartment. Chuck tells this short story of how he and Jason discover the culprit.

148. Fife, Dale. **North of Danger**. E.P. Dutton, 1978.
72 p. ISBN: 0-525-36035-2; GrL: 5-9; RdL: 4
Twelve-year-old Arne undertakes a 200-mile trip on skis in order to warn his father about a German invasion of their Norwegian town in Svalbard.

149. Fife, Dale. **Sesame Seed Snatchers**. Houghton Mifflin Company, 1983.
97 p. ISBN: 0-395-34826-9; GrL: 4-6; RdL: 4
During summer vacation, 10-year-old Mike and his best friend, Hank, form "The Two Guys Private Eyes" detective agency. Their first case involves seeds that disappear from a nearby factory. "Suky" Susannah Freebee leads them through.

150. Fleischman, Paul. **Phoebe Danger, Detective in the Case of the Two-Minute Cough**. Houghton Mifflin Company, 1983.
58 p. ISBN: 0-395-33226-5; GrL: 4-5; RdL: 3
Phoebe Dangerfield and her birdwatching friend, Dash, the sole members of the Phoebe Danger Detective Agency, take on their first case. A priceless antique medicine bottle and a postage stamp are missing from the Willingtons' collections. The sleuths discover the thief in record time.

151. Fleischman, Sid. **Bloodhound Gang in the Case of the Secret Message**. Random House, 1981.
62 p. ISBN: 0-394-84764-4; 0-394-94764-9 LB; GrL: 4-6; RdL: 4; OP
Published in conjunction with the Children's Television Workshop (3-2-1 Contact), the Bloodhound books are based on the television series of the same name. The detectives, Vikki, Ricardo, and Zach, combine their talents to solve a coded message that enables them to capture a diamond smuggler.

152. Fleischman, Sid. **McBroom Tells a Lie**. Little, Brown and Company, 1976.
46 p. ISBN: 0-316-28572-2; GrL: 2-5; RdL: 4
Josh McBroom admits to telling only one lie, but the reader will laugh at the outrageous circumstances that surround this farmer and his family. McBroom's soil is noted for growing amazing things. In this account, he and his children save the farm by using a popcorn-mobile and plenty of ingenuity.

153. Foley, June. **Love By Any Other Name**. Delacorte, 1983.
216 p. ISBN: 0-440-04865-6; GrL: 7-up; RdL: 3; OP
When 15-year-old Billie meets the considerate, brainy Cameron, she reconsiders her preference for the brawny, handsome sports star she's been going with. But she worries whether she will lose the popularity she's enjoyed if she makes the switch.

154. Foley, Louise Munro. **Tackle 22**. Delacorte/Dell, 1978/1981.
43 p. ISBN: 0-440-08465-2 LB; 0-440-48484-7 PB; GrL: 2-4; RdL: 2; OP
Herbie, Chub's little brother, fills in for a sick member of the Wildcats football team, much to his brother's dismay. The fun begins when Herbie tackles everything in sight, including a dog, garbage can, even a tree. He shapes up in time for the big game with the Spacemen and makes the game-saving tackle.

155. Franchere, Ruth. **Cesar Chavez**. Thomas Y. Crowell, 1973.
48 p. ISBN: 0-690-18385-2; 0-690-18384-4 LB; GrL: 4-6; RdL: 3
Story of the life and work of Cesar Chavez, founder of the National Farm Workers Union. He grew up a "Mexican-American," even though he was born in the United States. He labored to educate and to promote the rights of migrant workers who were impoverished and exploited.

156. Franklin, Lance. **Double Play**. Bantam (Varsity Coach Series), 1987.
135 p. ISBN: 0-553-26526-1; GrL: 6-up; RdL: 5; OP
Tom Keenan is a key player on a championship baseball team as well as a rock musician in a band with late-night club bookings. When the two activities create more pressure than he can handle and his schoolwork starts to suffer, he is faced with a serious decision—which one to choose.

157. Franklin, Lance. **Takedown**. Bantam (Varsity Coach Series), 1986.
138 p. ISBN: 0-553-26209-2 PB; GrL: 6-up; RdL: 4; OP
Kevin learns to believe in himself despite his home situation and his own growing addiction to alcohol through the efforts of wrestling Coach Cronin.

158. Gardiner, John Reynolds. **Top Secret**. Little, Brown and Company, 1984.
110 p. ISBN: 0-316-30368-2; GrL: 4-6; RdL: 3
Allen Brewster tells the incredible story of his theory of human photosynthesis. He is determined to prove, for his science fair project, that humans can convert sunlight into food for human blood cells. His classmates and his teacher jeer at him, but after trying out his theory, Allen turns green!

159. Gauch, Patricia Lee. **Aaron and the Green Mountain Boys**. Coward,
McCann and Geoghegan, 1972.
62 p. ISBN: 0; GrL: 1-4; RdL: 2; OP
Nine-year-old Aaron Robinson is not satisfied helping his grandfather bake
bread while others engage in physical combat with the British in a nearby
Vermont town. But he soon learns that their bread nourishes the troops who
then march on to victory.

160. Gauch, Patricia Lee. **Thunder at Gettysburg**. Coward, McCann and
Geoghegan, 1975.
46 p. ISBN: 0-698-20329-1 TR; 0-698-30582-5 LB; GrL: 4-6; RdL: 4; OP
Similar in format to Monjo's Vicksburg Veteran, this fictionalized account of
the battle that was the turning point of the Civil War features a female protag-
onist. Fourteen-year- old Tillie Pierce finds herself unexpectedly involved in
the struggle between Union and Rebel soldiers on a nearby farm.

161. Giff, Patricia Reilly. **Have You Seen Hyacinth Macaw?** Delacorte, 1981.
134 p. ISBN: 0-440-03467-1; 0-440-03472-8 LB; GrL: 4-6; RdL: 3
Junior Detective Abby and her friend, Potsie, work to solve several mysteries
that involve a new neighbor, a theft and the unusual actions of Abby's brother.

162. Giff, Patricia Reilly. **Powder Puff Puzzle**. Dell (Polka Dot Private Eye),
1987.
75 p. ISBN: 0-440-47180-X PB; GrL: 2-4; RdL: 1
Dawn Bosco, private eye, is on the case of the missing feline, Powder Puff,
who disappears when a car drives away with her. Others in the series: The
Mystery of the Blue Ring; The Riddle of the Red Purse; and The Secret of
the Polk Street School.

163. Giff, Patricia Reilly. **Ronald Morgan Goes to Bat**. Viking, Kestrel, 1988.
31 p. ISBN: 0-670-81457-1; GrL: 3-4; RdL: 1
Although he cannot hit or catch a ball, Ronald Morgan loves baseball. What
he has is a lot of spirit and with a little practice this may be all that he needs
to succeed at the game.

164. Giff, Patricia Reilly. **Say "Cheese"**. Dell (Kids of the Polk Street School),
1985.
79 p. ISBN: 0-440-47639-9; GrL: 4-6; RdL: 2
This simple story captures the spirit of the last days of school with a special
picnic outing where Emily Arrow learns the importance of having a variety
of friends. The story is told with lots of dialogue and some humor. There are
several other books in the series.

165. Giff, Patricia Reilly. **Suspect**. E.P. Dutton (A Skinny Book), 1982.
72 p. ISBN: 0-525-45108-0; GrL: 7-up; RdL: 1; OP
Paul Star unwillingly gets involved with a murder when an unknown
woman steals his wallet. He becomes the prime suspect after he discovers a
dead body and alerts the police. Now he must clear himself by finding the
real murderer before it's too late.

166. Giff, Patricia Reilly. **Watch Out, Ronald Morgan**. Viking, Kestrel, 1985.
25 p. ISBN: 0-670-80433-9; GrL: 1-3; RdL: 1
Ronald has many humorous mishaps until he gets a pair of eyeglasses.
There is a special note for adults about eyeglasses at the end of the book.

167. Gilson, Jamie. **Double Dog Dare**. Lothrop, Lee & Shepard, 1988.
126 p. ISBN: 0-688-07969-5; GrL: 3-6; RdL: 2
In this sequel to Thirteen Ways To Sink a Sub, Hobie Hanson invents ways
to dazzle his classmates when he returns from summer vacation to find that
all his other classmates have done incredible things—one has even won a
Preteen Personality contest—and he hasn't.

168. Girard, Ken. **Double Exposure**. Fearon (Fastback Spy), 1985.
30 p. ISBN: 0-8224-6539-6 PB; GrL: 9-up; RdL: 5
Frank Egan once helped the FBI, so they promise him a new life and a new
identity. But the terror begins when his new face brings an old nightmare as
different spies and agents come after him. One of 30 small-sized paperbacks
in the Fastback Spy series.

169. Glendinning, Sally. **Doll: Bottle-Nosed Dolphin**. Garrard, 1980.
38 p. ISBN: 0-8116-7501-7; GrL: 2-5; RdL: 3
Mildly anthropomorphized (but nonfiction) account of an Atlantic bottle-
nosed dolphin's life from birth to her new home in Marine World. Filled
with interesting facts about dolphins, it is mixed with a slight story line
about how this young dolphin and her mother came to perform in a sea
show.

170. Goodsell, Jane. **Eleanor Roosevelt**. Crowell, 1970.
38 p. ISBN: 0-690-25626-4; GrL: 2-4; RdL: 2
The story of this remarkable woman who became the wife of the thirty-sec-
ond president of the United States is told from her shy childhood to her
death.

171. Gorman, Carol. **Chelsey and the Green-Haired Kid**.
Houghton Mifflin Company, 1987.
110 p. ISBN: 0-395-41854-2; GrL: 7-9; RdL: 5
Jack, a punker, and Chelsey, a spunky paraplegic, team up to solve the murder of a teenager at a basketball game when everyone else thinks it was an
accident.

172. Gray, William R. **Camping Adventure**. National Geographic Society, 1976.
31 p. ISBN: 0-87044-196-5; GrL: 3-6; RdL: 2
Beautiful color photographs (typical of National Geographic Society) take up most of the book, which is thin and tall. This book portrays a family with young children going on an outdoor excursion. It tells how they prepare, what supplies they bring, how they cope with nature and some of the fun they have.

173. Greene, Carol. **Astronauts**. Childrens Press (New True Books), 1984.
45 p. ISBN: 0-516-01722-5; GrL: 3-6; RdL: 3
This is an introduction to the history of aeronautics, the astronauts, cosmonauts and what it's like to fly into space. Sally K. Ride and Guion Bluford are highlighted for their roles as the first American woman and the first black American in space.

174. Greene, Carol. **I Can Be a Baseball Player**. Childrens Press, 1985.
31 p. ISBN: 0-516-01845-0; GrL: 1-4; RdL: 2
This is one of a series of nonfiction introductions to various occupations, including teacher, computer operator, astronaut, and musician. This one gives a very simple but well done overview of the baseball profession. A chart at the beginning shows all the positions of the game.

175. Greene, Carol. **Jenny Summer**. Harper & Row, 1988.
76 p. ISBN: 0-06-022209-3 LB; GrL: 2-4; RdL: 2
In this sequel to Robin Hill, Robin is happy when she gets a new neighbor her age to play with during the summer. They become best friends but suddenly, when the girl has to move away, Robin feels the pain of lost friendship.

176. Greene, Janice. **Flight of the Sparrow**. Fearon (Fastback Spy), 1985.
30 p. ISBN: 0-8224-6540-X PB; GrL: 9-up; RdL: 4
Allan Traven of the British Intelligence Service meets Stepan Yevchenko of the KGB and must learn whether this Russian is defecting or a double agent. Stepan, the "Sparrow," must prove his loyalties before it's too late.

177. Greene, Shep. **Boy Who Drank Too Much**. Dell, 1979.
157 p. ISBN: 0-440-90493-5 PB; GrL: 6-up; RdL: 2
Fifteen-year-old Buff succumbs to pressures from his father to be a star ice hockey player, and to avoid his physically abusive father, Buff drinks. His close friends come to his aid before it's too late.

178. Greenwald, Sheila. **Valentine Rosy**. Little, Brown and Company, 1984.
89 p. ISBN: 0-316-32708-5; GrL: 3-5; RdL: 3
Eleven-year-olds Rosy and her friend, Hermione, have a Valentine's Day party against Rosy's will, just to compete with the popular Christi McCurry, who is also having a party that night.

179. Gutman, Bill. **Pro Football's Record Breakers**. Archway (Sports Illustrated), 1987.
121 p. ISBN: 0-671-64375-4 PB; GrL: 6-up; RdL: 6
Football's superstars, past and present, and the stories behind their successes are featured in this illustrated book. Players include Phil Simms, Dan Marino, Walter Payton, teams like the Steelers and more.

180. Gutman, Bill. **Smitty**. Turman Publishing Company, 1988.
78 p. ISBN: 0-89872-301-9 PB; GrL: 6-up; RdL: 4.
Valerie Smith, an all-star basketball senior, moves to a new school only to discover that there isn't any girls basketball team. Because she is in line for a college scholarship and must play, she decides to try out for the boys team and makes it!

181. Haas, Dorothy. **Secret Life of Dilly McBean**. Bradbury Press, 1986.
202 p. ISBN: 0-02-738200-1; GrL: 5-7; RdL: 4
Dilloway McBean, age 12, is an orphan who is wealthy and possesses an unusual power—he's magnetic. He keeps this a secret until he must use it to destroy the plans of the dastardly Dr. Keenwit, who seeks to control the world with a computer.

182. Haas, Dorothy. **To Catch a Crook**. Clarion, 1988.
101 p. ISBN: 0-89919-715-9; GrL: 4-6; RdL: 3
When Gabby O'Brien decides to be a private eye for Career Day at school, she finds herself in the middle of a rash of puzzling neighborhood thefts that put her skills to task.

183. Hall, Katy, and Lisa Eisenberg. **Buggy Riddles**. Dial, 1986.
48 p. ISBN: 0-8037-0140-3 LB; GrL: 2-4; RdL: 1
Colorful illustrations complement these 42 insect-related riddles and jokes.

184. Hall, Lynn. **Captain: Canada's Flying Pony**. Garrard, 1976.
64 p. ISBN: 0-8116-4857-5; GrL: 3-6; RdL: 3; OP
The story of a young rider and her warm relationship with the Canadian champion pony, Scots Greys Captain. Tracy takes riding lessons and befriends a spotted pony that is all alone in a pasture. She has great hopes of riding Captain one day— a day that comes sooner than she thinks.

185. Hall, Lynn. **If Winter Comes**. Charles Scribner's Sons, 1986.
119 p. ISBN: 0-684-18575-X; GrL: 6-up; RdL: 5
The meaning of life is a focal point of this realistic story of the threat of nuclear war. Two teenagers, Meredith and her boyfriend, Barry, draw closer together, with each other and with their families, despite their totally different reactions to what may be the last weekend of their lives.

186. Hallowell, Tommy. **Out of Bounds**. Bantam (Varsity Coach Series), 1987.
     124 p. ISBN: 0-553-26338-2 PB; GrL: 6-up; RdL: 5; OP
     A basketball fanatic and star player is forced off the team after an injury, and
     his only link to the team is the coach's offer of becoming the team's camera-
     man. But will this be enough for a player whose whole life is basketball?

187. Hallum, Red. **Kookie Rides Again**. Educational Activities, 1974.
     32 p. ISBN: 0-914296-19-1; GrL: 2-6; RdL: 4
     Kookie the dog is famous because he rides a motorcycle in races with his
     owner, John McCown. He and his master have ridden in over 200 desert
     races. In this book, the reader follows a race through the Mojave Desert.

188. Handford, Martin. **Find Waldo Now**. Little, Brown and Company, 1988.
     n.p. ISBN: 0-316-34292-0; GrL: 4-6; RdL: 6
     In this sequel to Where's Waldo?, the reader hunts for Waldo amid humor-
     ous historical scenes featuring Egyptians, Vikings and Romans. The brief
     text here is harder than the first book and includes different typefaces. But
     the real attraction is still the fun of searching for the backpacker.

189. Handford, Martin. **Where's Waldo?** Little, Brown and Company, 1987.
     n.p. ISBN: 0-316-34293-9; GrL: 3-6; RdL: 3
     The reader is invited to search for Waldo, a backpacker, on pages crammed
     with hundreds of people. Scenes include the beach, countryside, sporting
     events and the airport. After finding Waldo, the challenge is to return to
     each page and find the object that he has lost. The sequel: Find Waldo Now.

190. Harding, Lee. **Fallen Spaceman**. Bantam-Skylark, 1973.
     95 p. ISBN: 0-553-15147-9; GrL: 2-5; RdL: 3
     A boy is trapped in an alien's spaceship after it crashes to Earth, where the
     spaceman has little time to live. In this strange encounter, the courageous
     alien works to save the boy before it is too late for both of them.

191. Harris, Robie H. **Rosie's Double Dare**. Alfred A. Knopf, 1980.
     112 p. ISBN: 0-394-94459-3; 0-394-84459-9 PB; GrL: 3-6; RdL: 2
     Tired of being excluded from her brother's baseball gang, Rosie accepts two
     dares as a test. If she does what the group dares her to, then she'll be able to
     play ball with them. The challenges should get her into trouble, but she
     winds up with surprising good fortune.

192. Hart, Angela. **Dogs**. Franklin Watts, 1982.
     32 p. ISBN: 0-531-04446-7; GrL: 2-6; RdL: 3; OP
     Nonfiction presentation about different types of dogs, how the Canis family
     came to be, how to take care of puppies and other interesting information
     about dogs. It includes an index and color illustrations.

193. Hayward, Linda. **Hello, House!** Random House (Step Into Reading), 1988.
     32 p. ISBN: 0-394-88864-2 PB; 0-394-98864-7 LB; GrL: 1-3; RdL: 1
     An adaptation of the Uncle Remus tale "Heyo House" in which the clever
     Brer Rabbit outwits Brer Wolf once again.

194. Heide, Florence Parry. **Banana Twist**. Holiday House, 1978.
     111 p. ISBN: 0-8234-0334-3; GrL: 4-6; RdL: 4
     Hilarious story of Jonah D. Krock and his escapades with his neighbor,
     Goober Grube, the oddball. Jonah tells his schemes to elude Goober, but
     they're usually to no avail. At the end of the book, much to Jonah's dismay,
     his omnipresent pal even winds up going to the same boarding same board-
     ing school.

195. Heilbroner, Joan. **Meet George Washington**. Random House, 1964.
     86 p. ISBN: 0-394-80058-3; 0-394-90058-8 LB; GrL: 4-6; RdL: 2
     The emphasis in this account is on Washington's military duties that led up
     to his presidency, with brief mention of his life after holding this office. Its
     best features are the clarity in writing style, a good mixture of historical tid-
     bits and narrative.

196. Hildick, E.W. **Case of the Wandering Weathervanes**. Macmillan, 1988.
     152 p. ISBN: 0-02-743970-4; GrL: 4-6; RdL: 4
     The eighteenth in the McGurk Mystery series, this begins with weather-
     vanes disappearing—all kinds, all over town. McGurk and his group of
     investigators try to find them and why they've disappeared.

197. Hiller, B.B. **Karate Kid**. Scholastic, 1984.
     131 p. ISBN: 0-590-33306-2; GrL: 5-up; RdL: 5
     Based on the popular movie of the same name this is the story of Daniel,
     who has just moved from New Jersey to California and finds the living there
     very different. Here he is victimized by the toughest kid in his school until
     he learns karate from a man who teaches him even more about life.

198. Hinton, S.E. **Taming the Star Runner**. Delacorte, 1988.
     181 p. ISBN: 0-440-50058-3; GrL: 7-up; RdL: 6
     Travis moves to his uncle's horse farm after serving time in juvenile hall for
     assaulting his stepfather. There he tries to adjust to his new environment as
     well as new feelings about himself and his rage, which he channels into the
     writing of a novel.

199. Hinton, S.E. **That Was Then, This Is Now**. Viking, 1971.
     154 p. ISBN: 0-440-98652-4; GrL: 7-12; RdL: 6
     Bryon and Mark, childhood friends, are like brothers. This bond is broken
     when Bryon learns that Mark sells drugs to kids.

200. Hoff, Syd. **Horse in Harry's Room**. Harper & Row (Early I Can Read), 1970.
32 p. ISBN: 06-022482-7 TR; 06-022483-5 LB; GrL: 1-4; RdL: 1
Harry and his imaginary horse have a special understanding—that is, only Harry can see him. When his parents take Harry to to see real horses he learns that horses should be free. So, he is even more delighted when his horse decides to stay.

201. Hoff, Syd. **Stanley**. Harper & Row (I Can Read), 1962.
64 p. ISBN: 0-06-022536-X LB; 0-06-444010-9 PB; GrL: 1-3; RdL: 2
A good-natured caveman who likes to paint, plant seeds and befriend animals moves out of his cold cave and designs the world's first house.

202. Hooks, William H. **Pioneer Cat**. Random House (Stepping Stone Books), 1988.
63 p. ISBN: 0-394-82038-X PB; 0-394-92038-4 LB; GrL: 3-4; RdL: 2
Nine-year-old Kate Purdy travels with her family in a covered wagon from Missouri to Oregon. She sneaks a cat on board against her father's rules, but bringing Snuggs along turns out to be a good idea.

203. Hopkins, Lee Bennett, ed. **More Surprises**. Harper & Row, 1987.
64 p. ISBN: 0-060-226-056 LB; GrL: 1-4; RdL: Varies
Sequel to Surprises also by Hopkins, with the same variety and warmth found in the first volume of these easy-to-read beginning books of verse by American poets.

204. Hopkins, Lee Bennett, ed. **Surprises**. Harper & Row (I Can Read), 1984.
64 p. ISBN: 0-06-022585-8 LB; GrL: 1-4; RdL: Varies
Thirty-eight easy-to-read, short poems by American poets on a variety of pleasant subjects like pets and feelings. Poets include Langston Hughes, Karla Kuskin, Eve Merriam and more.

205. Howe, James. **Stage Fright**. Avon (A Sebastian Barth Mystery), 1987.
121 p. ISBN: 0-380-70173-1; GrL: 6-up; RdL: 4
Young sleuth Sebastian Barth returns to solve the mystery of who is trying to keep the curtain from going up on a summer stock drama that features a famous movie star.

206. Hurwitz, Johanna. **Adventures of Ali Baba Bernstein**. Morrow, 1985.
96 p. ISBN: 0-688-04161-2; 0-688-04345-3 LB; GrL: 4-6; RdL: 4
David decides all his life will be more adventurous when he changes his name to Ali Baba ... and it is. He discovers a jewel thief in his apartment building, has other funny episodes and winds up inviting all of the David Bernstein's in the Manhattan telephone book to his birthday party.

207. Hurwitz, Johanna. **Aldo Applesauce**. Morrow/Scholastic, 1979.
127 p. ISBN: 0-688-32199-2 LB; 0-590-33751-3 PB; GrL: 3-5; RdL: 3
Aldo and his family move from New York City to a suburb in New Jersey.
He adjusts pretty well to his environs, but has trouble making friends in
school. To make matters worse, he inadvertently gets the nickname "Applesauce" when his spills in the cafeteria.

208. Jones, Betty Millsaps. **Wonder Women of Sports**. Random House (Step-
Up Books), 1981.
72 p. ISBN: 0-394-94475-5 LB; 0-394-84475-0 PB; GrL: 4-8; RdL: 3
This collection of one dozen stories of women athletes includes Nadia
Comaneci, Billie Jean King and Sonja Henie. It is easy to read and includes
photographs.

209. Kalb, Jonah. **Easy Baseball Book**. Houghton Mifflin Company, 1976.
49 p. ISBN: 0-395-24385-8; GrL: 2-5; RdL: 2
This is part of a series of practical books showing baseball techniques,
equipment, and how to improve hitting, throwing and other skills. It also
includes common mistakes made and ways to correct them. Others in the
series are: The Easy Hockey Book and The Easy Ice Skating Book.

210. Kalb, Jonah. **Easy Hockey Book**. Houghton Mifflin Company, 1977.
64 p. ISBN: 0-395-25842-1; GrL: 2-5; RdL: 2
Part of the series that includes The Easy Baseball Book and The Easy Skating Book. See preceding entry for The Easy Baseball Book.

211. Kalb, Jonah. **Easy Ice Skating Book**. Houghton Mifflin Company, 1981.
64 p. ISBN: 0-395-31605-7; GrL: 2-5; RdL: 2
Part of the series which includes: The Easy Baseball Book and The Easy
Hockey Book. See entry under Kalb, Jonah, The Easy Baseball Book.

212. Kalb, Jonah. **Goof That Won the Pennant**. Houghton Mifflin Company,
1976.
103 p. ISBN: 0-395-24834-5; GrL: 3-6; RdL: 4
The Blazers, a group of outcasts who don't usually take their game seriously, begin to thirst for victory as they take advantage of a once-in-a-lifetime
error during a baseball game.

213. Kassem, Lou. **Middle School Blues**. Houghton Mifflin Company, 1986.
181 p. ISBN: 0-395-39499-6; GrL: 5-8; RdL: 2
Cindy, who is 12, starts seventh grade uneasily. She goes to the library to
find a book to help her cope with her new situation and finds none. So she
starts to write one of her own with her friend. She soon learns that these new
experiences can be quite enjoyable.

214. Kessler, Leonard. **Old Turtle's Baseball Stories**. Greenwillow (Read-Alone), 1982.
55 p. ISBN: 0-688-00723-6; 0-688-00724-4 LB; GrL: 1-3; RdL: 1
While gathered around the wood stove, Old Turtle tells his friends some unbelievable baseball stories.

215. Kessler, Leonard. **Old Turtle's Riddle and Joke Book**. Greenwillow (Read-Alone), 1986.
47 p. ISBN: 0-688-05954-6 LB; GrL: 1-3; RdL: 1
Old Turtle writes his own joke book with the help of his friends dog, cat, duck, frog, chicken, owl and gull, who contribute riddles about animals.

216. Kessler, Leonard. **Old Turtle's Soccer Team**. Greenwillow (Read-Alone), 1988.
47 p. ISBN: 0-688-07157-0; 0-688-07158-9 LB; GrL: 1-4; RdL: 1
Animals learn to play soccer and the meaning of good sportsmanship under Old Turtle's guidance.

217. Kessler, Leonard. **On Your Mark, Get Set, Go!** Harper & Row, 1972.
63 p. ISBN: 06-023152-1; 06-023153-X; GrL: K-4; RdL: 1; OP
An all-animal Olympics has been planned and everyone has a spot except worm, who anxiously awaits on the sidelines. But worm's moment arrives when she wiggles ahead to win for her team.

218. Kibbe, Pat. **Hocus-Pocus Dilemma**. Alfred A. Knopf/Apple Paperbacks, 1979/1982.
124 p. ISBN: 0-394-94058-X LB; 0-590-30093-8 PB; GrL: 4-6; RdL: 4
Ten-year-old B.J. has ESP — or so she believes in this humorous story of family life. It's packed with mishaps when B.J. gets hold of some fortune-telling books and a crystal ball. When she thinks she can predict the outcome of events, she becomes more of a bother than a seer.

219. King, P.E. **Down on the Funny Farm**. Random House (Step Into Reading), 1986.
48 p. ISBN: 0-394-87460-9 TR; 0-394-97460-3 LB; GrL: 1-3; RdL: 1
A farmer thinks he is getting a real bargain when he buys a farm for one dollar, until he finds out that all the animals are confused about what they are supposed to do.

220. Kline, Suzy. **Herbie Jones**. Putnam Publishing Group, 1985.
95 p. ISBN: 0-399-21183-7; GrL: 3-4; RdL: 3
Herbie and his best friend, Raymond, share many third-grade adventures: both are in the lowest reading group and are sick of it; both attend a surprising boy/girl birthday party; both wonder if there are really ghosts in the girls bathroom at school.

221. Kline, Suzy. **Herbie Jones and the Class Gift**. Putnam Publishing Group, 1987.
94 p. ISBN: 0-399-21452-6; GrL: 3-5; RdL: 3
Disaster strikes when Herbie and his friend, Raymond, accidentally break their teacher's gift. But with some fast thinking they come up with a plan to save themselves and the gift that will surprise everyone. But what they don't know is that a surprise is in store for them.

222. Kline, Suzy. **Herbie Jones and the Monster Ball**. Putnam Publishing Group, 1988.
126 p. ISBN: 0-399-21569-7; GrL: 3-5; RdL: 3
Herbie Jones, also known as a Strikeout King, feels that his summer's already ruined when his uncle arrives as the new coach of a baseball team and asks Herbie to join in this sequel to Herbie Jones and the Class Gift.

223. Kraske, Robert. **Magicians Do Amazing Things**. Random House (Step-Up Books), 1979.
69 p. ISBN: 0-394-84106-9; 0-394-94106-3 LB; GrL: 3-6; RdL: 2; OP
Highlights "impossible" tricks by six famous magicians. These include Raymond Saunders, Harry Houdini, Chung Ling Soo, Harry Kellar, Jean-Eugene Robert-Houdin, and Howard Thurston. The author allows the reader to try and guess the solution to the tricks. Correct answers are in the back of the book.

224. Krementz, Jill. **How It Feels to Be Adopted**. Alfred A. Knopf, 1982.
107 p. ISBN: 0-394-52851-4; 0-394-75853-6 PB; GrL: 3-up; RdL: Varies
Children ages 8 through 16 tell their feelings about being adopted children. Part of a series that includes: How It Feels When a Parent Dies and How It Feels When Parents Divorce. Illustrated with black-and-white photographs and includes an introduction by Krementz.

225. Krementz, Jill. **How It Feels When a Parent Dies**. Alfred A. Knopf, 1988.
110 p. ISBN: 0-394-51911-6; 0-394-75854-4 PB; GrL: 3-up; RdL: Varies
Eighteen children ages 7 through 16 share their thoughts, in their own words, about losing a parent. With black- and-white photographs. Others in the series: How It Feels to Be Adopted and How It Feels When Parents Divorce. Includes an introduction by Krementz on the the topic.

226. Krementz, Jill. **How It Feels When Parents Divorce**. Alfred A. Knopf, 1984.
115 p. ISBN: 0-394-54079-4; 0-394-75855-2 PB; GrL: 3-up; RdL: varies
Nineteen children ages 7 to 16 share their reactions, fears about their parents' divorce. With black-and-white photos and an introduction by Krementz. Others in the series: How It Feels To Be Adopted and How It Feels When A Parent Dies.

227. Krensky, Stephen. **Lionel in the Fall**. Dial (Easy-To-Read), 1987.
   48 p. ISBN: 0-8037-0384-8; 0-8037-0385-6 LB; GrL: 1-3; RdL: 2
   For Lionel this time of year is a special one. Fall means a new teacher and a
   new school year, raking leaves and jumping in them and the thrills of Halloween night.

228. Kuklin, Susan. **Taking My Cat to the Vet**. Bradbury Press, 1988.
   n.p. ISBN: 0-02-751233-9; GrL: K-3; RdL: 2
   Ben takes his cat, Willa, to the vet for an exam. There, he watches and learns
   about health problems a cat might have, what a vet does and how he can
   take care of his pet. Full-color pictures accompany this essay. In the back of
   the book is a list of tips for a successful visit to the veterinarian.

229. Landon, Lucinda. **Meg Mackintosh and the Case of the Missing Babe
   Ruth Baseball**. Atlantic Monthly Press, 1986.
   48 p. ISBN: 0-87113-055-6; GrL: 2-4; RdL: 2
   A young female sleuth solves the mystery of her grandfather's baseball,
   autographed by Babe Ruth, that has been missing since 1928. She cleverly
   puts together clues, found in an old family scrapbook, that were left by the
   culprit-cousin who hid the ball in the first place.

230. Larrick, Nancy. **Cats Are Cats**. Philomel Books, 1988.
   80 p. ISBN: 0-399-21517-4; GrL: All ages; RdL: Varies
   Forty-two poems by various poets about all kinds of cats: proud ones,
   funny ones, beautiful ones, mischievous ones, all shown with beautiful illustrations by Ed Young.

231. Latham, Jean Lee. **Elizabeth Blackwell: Pioneer Woman Doctor**. Garrard,
   1975.
   80 p. ISBN: 0-8116-6319-1; GrL: 3-6; RdL: 3; OP
   Biography of the first woman doctor in the United States, who helped combat disease as she advanced the cause of women in the medical profession.

232. Lauber, Patricia. **Snakes Are Hunters**. Crowell (Let's Read & Find Out...),
   1988.
   32 p. ISBN: 0-690-04628-6; 0-690-04630-8 LB; GrL: 1-4; RdL: 2
   Describes the physical characteristics of a variety of snakes and how they
   hunt, catch and eat their prey. With color illustrations.

233. Law, Carol Russell. **Case of the Weird Street Firebug**. Alfred A. Knopf,
   1980.
   118 p. ISBN: 0-394-84480-7 PB; GrL: 4-6; RdL: 3
   Steffi Bradley is an aspiring detective who gets firsthand experience after
   she enrolls in a mail-order detective school. One of her first lessons is tailing
   suspicious-looking people; this gets her involved accidently with solving
   the mystery of the arsonist who has been setting fires throughout her town.

234. Laymon, Richard. **Cobra**. Fearon (Fastback Spy), 1985.
28 p. ISBN: 0-8224-6535-3 PB; GrL: 9-up; RdL: 5
Undercover cop Blake Douglas has only one chance to bust a terrorist group and that's to become their top assassin. But he doesn't count on falling for a beautiful but deadly group member.

235. LeSieg, Theo. **Wacky Wednesday**. Random House, 1974.
n.p. ISBN: 0-394-82912-3 TR; 0-394-92912-8 LB; GrL: 1-3; RdL: 1
It all begins when a youngster wakes up to find a shoe on the wall. All sorts of unusual things happen on this silly day.

236. Leslie-Melville, Betty. **Daisy Rothschild, The Giraffe That Lives with Me**. Doubleday, 1987.
41 p. ISBN: 0-385-23895-9; 0-385-23896-7 LB; GrL: 4-8; RdL: 6
Saved from poachers, this Rothschild giraffe is raised in captivity by the author. The moving story of how she was saved and her new life in Kenya is shared in color photos and moving language.

237. Levine, Ellen. **Secret Missions: Four True Life Stories**. Scholastic, 1988.
116 p. ISBN: 0-590-41183-7 PB; GrL: 3-6; RdL: 4
The stories of four courageous individuals: Lydia Darragh, a Quaker housewife spy during the American Revolution; Alexander M. Ross, a Canadian who helped slaves escape; William Still, a son of slaves who kept secret Underground Rail- road logbooks; and Leesha Bos, a Jewish nurse who hid people from Nazies.

238. Levoy, Myron. **Shadow Like a Leopard**. New American Library (Signet), 1981.
137 p. ISBN: 0-451-13698-5 PB; GrL: 6-up; RdL: 3; OP
When Ramon robs an elderly painter he inadvertently opens himself to a strange new relationship when the old man befriends him. This has-been artist shows a street-wise kid a creative way to channel his need to be macho in a switchblade world.

239. Levy, Elizabeth. **Case of the Gobbling Squash**. Simon & Schuster (A Magic Mystery), 1988.
49 p. ISBN: 0-671-63655-3; GrL: 2-5; RdL: 3
A young detective and her amateur magician partner solve a case involving missing rabbits, a ghost and a remote control squash that gobbles like a turkey. As a bonus, the book includes how to do magic tricks.

240. Levy, Elizabeth. **Cold As Ice**. Morrow, 1988.
167 p. ISBN: 0-688-06579-1; GrL: 6-9; RdL: 4
Kelly, who works in a sports arena, meets two competitive male skaters whose lives are threatened by mysterious accidents.

241. Levy, Elizabeth. **Dani Trap**. Avon/Flare, 1984.
     106 p. ISBN: 0-380-69995-8; GrL: 6-up; RdL: 3
     Danielle goes undercover to help police catch liquor-store owners who sell
     to minors. But she gets caught in a set-up, sending her to jail for attempted
     robbery.

242. Levy, Elizabeth. **Frankenstein Moved In on the Fourth Floor**. Harper &
     Row, 1979.
     57 p. ISBN: 0-06-023810-0; 0-06-023811-9 LB; GrL: 3-5; RdL: 4
     In this apartment-house suspense story, two boys suspect their weird neigh-
     bor is none other than Frankenstein! Sam and Robert decide to prove their
     suspicions by spying on him and by checking off a list of the monster's
     characteristics that match the neighbor's.

243. Levy, Elizabeth. **Running Out of Magic with Houdini**. Alfred A. Knopf,
     1981.
     119 p. ISBN: 0-394-94685-5 LB; 0-394-84685-0 PB; GrL: 4-6; RdL: 3; OP
     Nina, Francie and Bill are warming up for their run in the New York City
     Marathon when a dense fog transports them back to 1912. They arrive just
     in time to witness one of Houdini's death-defying rehearsals. Later they
     save his life when several con artists they have exposed try to murder the
     escape artist.

244. Levy, Elizabeth. **Something Queer at the Ballpark**. Dell, 1984.
     48 p. ISBN: 0-440-48116-3; GrL: 2-4; RdL: 2
     Gwen captures the culprit who stole Jill's lucky baseball bat. This slim
     book has colorful, cartoonlike drawings. Others in the series are Something
     Queer at the Library, Something Queer is Going On, Something Queer at
     the Haunted School, and Something Queer on Vacation.

245. Lewis, Marjorie. **Wrongway Applebaum**. Coward, McCannand and
     Geoghegan, 1984.
     63 p. ISBN: 0-698-20610-X; GrL: 4-6; RdL: 4
     Fifth-grade Stanley ("Applebaum") is always the last one to be chosen for
     the baseball team. When he gets a chance to be a part of the team, he's afraid
     of getting hit by the ball as it's pitched to him. Stanley becomes a hero
     when, because of his fast running, he ties the championship game.

246. Lobel, Arnold. **Frog and Toad Together**. Harper & Row (I Can Read),
     1971.
     64 p. ISBN: 06-023959-X TR; 06-023960-3 LB; GrL: K-3; RdL: 1
     Five short, humorous tales of two close friends. Some themes include
     patience while waiting for a garden to grow, and moderation by trying to
     stop eating cookies.

247. Lopshire, Robert. **How to Make Snop Snappers and Other Fine Things**. Greenwillow, 1977.
54 p. ISBN: 0-688-84066-3; GrL: K-4; RdL: 1; OP
Twenty-three easy-to-make games, toys and other fun projects using household supplies.

248. Lorimer, Janet. **Time's Reach**. Fearon (Bestellers), 1988.
60 p. ISBN: 0-8224-5338-X PB; GrL: 9-up; RdL: 3
Gail Crandall, while visiting her brother in Hawaii, meets the mysterious but attractive Colin Walker only to find out that he is a time traveler from the future.

249. Lowry, Lois. **Anastasia Again!** Houghton Mifflin Company, 1981.
145 p. ISBN: 0-395-31147-0; GrL: 4-6; RdL: 3
Twelve-year old Anastasia returns in this sequel to Anastasia Krupnik. She is horrified to learn that her family is giving up city life to move to the suburbs.

250. Luenn, Nancy. **Unicorn Crossing**. Atheneum, 1987.
51 p. ISBN: 0-689-31384-5; GrL: 3-5; RdL: 3
Jenny longs to see a real unicorn during her family's vacation. She gets encouragement from a kind old Mrs. Donovan while they pick roses together. When she does see a group of unicorns one misty morning, she wonders if they are real.

251. Madden, John. **First Book of Football**. Crown, 1988.
90 p. ISBN: 0-517-56981-7; GrL: 6-up; RdL: 4
Football and television commentator John Madden explains the fundamentals of football telling what makes it great and ways to appreciate the game while watching it.

252. Madison, Arnold. **Great Unsolved Cases**. Dell, 1978.
88 p. ISBN: 0-440-93099-5; GrL: 6-up; RdL: 3; OP
Three famous crime cases that have not been solved, including Jack the Ripper, the kidnapping of the Lindbergh baby and the bombing of Flight 967. Clues are given and the reader is invited to draw his or her own conclusions.

253. Malone, Mary. **Annie Sullivan**. Putnam (See & Read Biography), 1971.
61 p. ISBN: 0-399-60031-0; GrL: 2-4; RdL: 3; OP
Short version of the story of Annie Sullivan, who is better known as Hellen Keller's teacher. Illustrated with blue-and- brown sketches.

254. Manes, Stephen. **Boy Who Turned into a TV Set**. Coward, McCann & Geoghegan/Avon, 1979.
32 p. ISBN: 0-380-62000-6 PB; GrL: 2-5; RdL: 4
Imagine what would happen if a TV fanatic actually turned into a TV! In Ogden Pettibone's case, it's true. Not much happens, except that the set is turned on and off via belly button and Ogden gets into some pretty unusual situations because of his predicament.

255. Manes, Stephen. **Hooples' Haunted House**. Delacorte/Dell, 1981/1983.
    107 p. ISBN: 0-440-03736-0 LB; 0-440-43794-6 PB; GrL: 4-6; RdL: 3;
    OP
    Alvin Hoople convinces his parents that they should have a haunted house
    in their garage after the garage of the neighbors (who used to host this annu-
    al event) explodes. He gets his friends together and they turn a doomed Hal-
    loween into a festive one, complete with eerie haunted house.

256. Markle, Sandra. **Science Mini-Mysteries**. Atheneum, 1988.
    64 p. ISBN: 0-689-312-911; GrL: 4-6; RdL: Varies
    Contains easy-to-do experiments that invite the reader to guess the solutions
    or conclusions of each of the 29 scientific tricks and effects.

257. Martin, Ann M. **Just a Summer Romance**. Holiday House, 1987.
    163 p. ISBN: 0-8234-0649-0; GrL: 6-9; RdL: 3
    Melanie's first love is a handsome boy she meets at a beach resort during
    summer vacation. However, when school starts Melanie realizes it was just
    a summer fling. But when she sees Justin's face on People magazine and
    discovers he's a new television star, she makes a bold effort to contact him.

258. Marzollo, Jean. **Red Ribbon Rosie**. Random House (Stepping Stone
    Books), 1988.
    60 p. ISBN: 0-394-89608-4 PB; 0-394-99608-9 LB; GrL: 2-4; RdL: 3
    Rosie is tired of coming in second place in running competitions, so she
    decides to cheat. She beats her friend, Sally, which ruins their friendship.
    Rosie learns a valuable lesson about winning races and keeping her friends
    with the help of her older sister.

259. Marzollo, Jean, and Claudio Marzollo. **Jed and the Space Bandits**.
    Dial, 1987.
    48 p. ISBN: 0-8037-0135-7; 0-8037-0136-5 LB; GrL: 1-3; RdL: 2
    Jed, his teddy-bear robot and his pet "cogs" make up the Junior Space
    Patrol. Together they fight crime in the galaxy, flying his spaceship, Ace. In
    this episode, they meet Molly and try to free her parents, who have been
    captured by the evil space bandits.

260. Mazer, Harry. **Girl of His Dreams**. Thomas Y. Crowell, 1987.
    214 p. ISBN: 0-690-04642-1 LB; GrL: 7-up; RdL: 2
    In this sequel to The War on Villa Street, Willis Pierce has graduated high
    school and is looking to meet the perfect girl. When he meets Sophie there
    is an attraction, but she isn't exactly the one he imagined she'd be.

261. Mazer, Harry. **Snow Bound**. Dell, 1973.
    142 p. ISBN: 0-440-96134-3 PB; GrL: 6-up; RdL: 5
    Two antagonistic teenagers trapped in the wilderness during a winter storm
    learn how they must cooperate to survive after the car they were driving
    crashes in the woods.

262. Mazer, Harry. **War on Villa Street**. Dell, 1988.
     182 p. ISBN: 0-440-99062-9 PB; GrL: 7-up; RdL: 5
     Willis Pierce deals with the pressures around him: his father's drinking binges and a local gang's antagonism, by running away from these situations. When he starts coaching a mentally handicapped classmate, his self-esteem builds and he begins to face the world around him.

263. Mazer, Harry. **When the Phone Rang**. Scholastic, 1985.
     181 p. ISBN: 0-590-40383-4 PB; GrL: 6-up; RdL: 3
     After their parents die in a plane crash, Billy and his brother and sister try to pick up the pieces of their shattered lives, tackling the good and the bad, like his sister's new shoplifting problem.

264. Mazer, Norma Fox. **Up in Seth's Room**. Dell, 1979.
     199 p. ISBN: 0-440-99190-0 PB; GrL: 6-up; RdL: 3
     Fifteen-year-old Finn has choices to make when she falls in love with the nineteen-year-old loner, Seth. When her parents forbid her to see him she goes against their wishes for the first time in her life. She learns that sticking to her convictions can be liberating but painful.

265. Miles, Betty. **Secret Life of the Underwear Champ**. Alfred A. Knopf, 1981.
     117 p. ISBN: 0-394-84563-3 PB; GrL: 3-5; RdL: 2
     Larry becomes a television celebrity when he is discovered as a natural while in New York City. But his excitement wanes when he learns that he will be modeling underwear for a commercial.

266. Milton, Hilary. **Mayday! Mayday!** Franklin Watts, 1979.
     152 p. ISBN: 0-531-02890-9; GrL: 6-up; RdL: 5; OP
     After their airplane crashes, 11-year-old Allison and 14-year-old Mark try to make their way down a mountain to get help for the injured. They are frightened and followed by a pack of wild dogs. Only their courage and stamina keep them going.

267. Monjo, Ferdinand N. **Vicksburg Veteran**. Simon & Schuster, 1971.
     62 p. ISBN: 0-6716-5156-0; GrL: 3-6; RdL: 2; OP
     Thirteen-year-old Fred Grant accompanies his father, General Ulysses, on the campaign to capture Vicksburg, one of the most decisive battles of the Civil War. Fred tells this fictionalized account in diary form beginning with April 16 and ending on Independence Day 1863.

268. Montgomery, Elizabeth R. **Mystery of the Boy Next Door**. Garrard (For Real Series), 1978.
     48 p. ISBN: 0-8116-6400-7; GrL: 2-4; RdL: 1; OP
     Neighborhood children think the new boy next door is unfriendly when he does not want to play with them, until they discover that he is deaf and only communicates through sign language. Very easy book to read. Sign language chart is included.

269. Moore, Allan. **British Are Coming**. Fearon (War Flashback), 1987.
     29 p. ISBN: 0-8224-2924-1 PB; GrL: 9-up; RdL: 4
     Nineteen-year-old Zack is frightened while in battle fighting the British
     army but learns to overcome his paralyzing fear just in time.

270. Morressy, John. **Drought on Ziax II**. Walker & Company, 1978.
     77 p. ISBN: 0-8027-6315-4; 0-8027-6316-2 LB; GrL: 3-5; RdL: 3
     Toren Mallixxan and Rilmat, his friend, try to find a way to end a drought
     that is destroying their planet.

271. Morressy, John. **Humans of Ziax II**. Walker & Company, 1974.
     62 p. ISBN: 0-8027-6187-9; 0-8027-6316-2 LB; GrL: 4-6; RdL: 3
     Toren is a prisoner on a foreign planet. He is nursed back to health, after
     falling from an aircraft, by the Imbur creatures, who are similar to Earth-
     lings but pacifists. Young Toren learns the peaceful ways of these creatures,
     and when he is finally reunited with his father, he shares his newfound
     knowledge.

272. Morris, Robert A. **Seahorse**. Harper & Row (Science I Can Read), 1972.
     60 p. ISBN: 06-024338-4 TR; 06-024339-2 LB; GrL: 2-4; RdL: 1
     The unique role of the male seahorse in the life cycle is presented as well as
     what they eat, how they protect themselves and other interesting characteris-
     tics of these sea creatures.

273. Myers, Walter Dean. **Fallen Angels**. Scholastic Hardcover, 1988.
     309 p. ISBN: 0-590-40942-5; GrL: 9-up; RdL: 2
     A gripping account of a 17-year-old who enlists for active combat in Viet-
     nam. He spends a devastating year participating in the horrors of war with
     other young people his age. Written as a testament to the young adults who
     fought and died, this is a graphic but moving novel.

274. Myers, Walter Dean. **Hoops**. Dell, 1983.
     183 p. ISBN: 0-440-93884-8 PB; GrL: 7-up; RdL: 4
     Lonnie Jackson could be a basketball pro, and in the Tournament of Cham-
     pions he may have a chance to make it. But heavy betters want him and the
     coach to throw the game. As the last seconds tick Lonnie's future is on the
     line.

275. Nixon, Joan Lowery. **Seance**. Dell, 1980.
     172 p. ISBN: 0-440-97937-4 PB; GrL: 6-up; RdL: 3
     During a seance, Sara disappears and is later found murdered. Soon another
     girl is found dead. Lauren wonders if she will be next as she tries to solve
     the mystery before it's too late for her.

276. Nourse, Alan E. **Teen Guide to Birth Control**. Franklin Watts, 1988.
62 p. ISBN: 0-531-10625-X LB; GrL: 6-up; RdL: 6
Part of the Teen Guides series, this book explains what birth control is and various up-to-date devices and methods that can be used. Includes a glossary and an index.

277. Nourse, Alan E. **Teen Guide to Safe Sex**. Franklin Watts, 1988.
62 p. ISBN: 0-531-10592-X LB; GrL: 6-up; RdL: 6
Up-to-date discussion of sexually transmitted diseases (STD'S) including venereal diseases, genital herpes and AIDS. With a glossary, index and some pronunciation guides. Part of the Teen Guides series.

278. O'Connor, Dick. **Foul Play**. Fearon (SporTellers), 1981.
60 p. ISBN: 0-8224-6477-2 PB; GrL: 9-up; RdL: 4
Dave Stennis threw a game once for a gambling circle and now he's trapped in a racket and cannot get out.

279. O'Connor, Jim, and Jane O'Connor. **Ghost in Tent 19**. Random House (Stepping Stone Books), 1988.
62 p. ISBN: 0-394-89800-1 PB; 0-394-99800-6 LB; GrL: 4-6; RdL: 3
Four boys at camp find an old map resembling Captain Blood's treasure map. Suddenly one night, a ghostly boy appears to them and pleads for their help. He leads them in the search for buried pirate treasure.

280. Orgel, Doris. **Whiskers Once and Always**. Viking, 1986.
82 p. ISBN: 0-670-80959-4; GrL: 3-5; RdL: 2
When Becky's cat, Whiskers, dies she first reacts with anger that even gets her into trouble at school. But soon she comes to accept her loss and pays a final tribute to her pet.

281. Packard, Edward. **Sunken Treasure**. Bantam/Skylark (Choose Your Own Adventure), 1982.
52 p. ISBN: 0-553-05018-4; 0-553-15150-9 PB; GrL: 4-6; RdL: 2
In this larger-print, slimmer one of the series, a young lass (you, the reader) lives in Boston in 1793. You find an old map and desire to find out whether it is a real treasure map. As you search for buried treasure, you try to avoid danger and even death. (Choose Your Own Adventure series)

282. Parish, Peggy. **Clues in the Woods**. Macmillan/Dell, 1968/1980.
154 p. ISBN: 0-02-769880-7; 0-440-41461-X PB; GrL: 1-4; RdL: 2
Three young sleuths are visiting their grandparents who live near the woods. Scraps of garbage have been disappearing, as well as a red sweater. Liza, Bill and Jed decide to solve this slight mystery. Other plot lines include the acquisition of a new puppy and two runaways.

283. Parish, Peggy. **No More Monsters for Me!** Harper & Row (I Can Read), 1981.
     64 p. ISBN: 0-06-024657-X TR; 0-06-024658-8 LB; GrL: 1-4; RdL: 1
     Minneapolis Simpkin isn't allowed to have a pet, but she finds a most unusual replacement—a baby monster that she hides in the basement. To her surprise it grows bigger every hour!

284. Parish, Peggy. **Too Many Rabbits.** Macmillan (Ready-To-Read), 1974.
     48 p. ISBN: 0-02-769850-5; GrL: 1-3; RdL: 1; OP
     A kind woman opens her front door and her heart to a fat rabbit. The next day discovers baby bunnies all over her house. She decides to keep them until she learns that they keep multiplying until she finds a new home for them.

285. Park, Barbara. **Almost Starring Skinnybones.** Alfred A. Knopf, 1988.
     108 p. ISBN: 0-394-99831-6 LB; 0-394-89831-1 TR; GrL: 3-6; RdL: 3
     In this funny sequel to Skinnybones, 12-year-old Alex is convinced that he will be a star when he wins a cat-food essay contest and is asked to make a television commercial.

286. Park, Barbara. **Don't Make Me Smile.** Alfred A. Knopf, 1981.
     114 p. ISBN: 0-394-84978-7; 0-394-94978-1; GrL: 4-6; RdL: 3
     Charlie Hinkle decides he would rather live in a tree when his parents tell him they are getting a divorce. Luckily, he finds a new friend to help him through the ordeal.

287. Park, Barbara. **Skinnybones.** Alfred A. Knopf, 1982.
     112 p. ISBN: 0-394-84988-4; 0-394-94988-9 LB; GrL: 4-6; RdL: 4
     Hilarious account of the madcap adventures of a boy who always gets the uniform that is way too big, the trophy for the Most Improved Player of the year, and into other hopeless situations. The big challenge is a pitching contest against one of the best ever to come along.

288. Patterson, Francine. **Koko's Kitten.** Scholastic, 1985.
     32 p. ISBN: 0-590-33811-0; GrL: 2-6; RdL: 3
     A true-life story of a gorilla in California who uses sign language. It tells of the relationship she had with a little kitten, All Ball, whom she loved and grieved over when it died. The large format is filled with excellent color photographs with single-line captions.

289. Paulsen, Gary. **Hatchet.** Bradbury Press, 1987.
     195 p. ISBN: 0-02-770130-1; GrL: 8-up; RdL: 7
     Thirteen-year-old Brian Robeson spends almost two months in the wilderness after his plane crashes. He learns to survive with only the hatchet that his mother has given him. And in doing so learns to live with his parents' new divorce.

290. Paulsen, Gary. **Tracker**. Bradbury Press, 1984/87.
90 p. ISBN: 0-14-032240-X PB; GrL: 6-up; RdL: 3
John Borne, age 13, used to love deer hunting with his grandfather, but now that his grandfather is dying of cancer John must hunt alone. When he tracks a doe and is unable to kill her, he comes to a new realization about life and death.

291. Petersen, David. **Airplanes**. Childrens Press (New True Books), 1981.
45 p. ISBN: 0-516-01606-7; GrL: 3-6; RdL: 3
Well-written introduction to numerous types of airplanes describes the type of things they are capable of doing. It provides some historical background, tells how airplanes fly and gives short descriptions of what a pilot does. There are good layouts with a photograph on almost every page.

292. Peterson, John. **How to Write Codes and Send Secret Messages**. Scholastic, 1966.
64 p. GrL: 3-5; RdL: 2; OP
This paperback includes simple techniques for fooling friends and keeping private messages from enemies by using household items. Space code messages, hidden words code, plus Greek codes and invisible ink, are explained.

293. Peterson, John. **Littles' Surprise Party**. Scholastic, 1972.
96 p. ISBN:; GrL: 2-5; RdL: 4; OP
Very popular story of the tiny family that lives in the Biggs' house. They are only a few inches tall and look human except for the little tail in the back. Similar to the Borrowers by Mary Norton (Harcourt Brace Jovanovich, 1975), the Littles get supplies and food from the castaways of the host family.

294. Pevsner, Stella. **And You Give Me a Pain, Elaine**. Houghton Mifflin Company, 1978.
182 p. ISBN: 0-395-28877-0; GrL: 4-6; RdL: 3
Andrea feels that her parents unfairly focus most of their attention and affections on her troublemaking older sister until tragedy strikes and the family must pull together.

295. Pevsner, Stella. **Sister of the Quints**. Clarion, 1987.
177 p. ISBN: 0-89919-498-2; GrL: 6-9; RdL: 2
Thirteen-year-old Natalie Wentworth tolerates her new family of quintuplets when her father remarries but realizes she needs to move in with her own mother to maintain her own identity.

296. Pfeffer, Susan Beth. **Kid Power**. Franklin Watts, 1977.
121 p. ISBN: 0-531-00123-7; GrL: 4-6; RdL: 4
Eleven-year-old Janice needs cash so she advertises her eagerness to do odd jobs around the neighborhood. She gets so much business that she hires her friends to help and becomes manager of the very successful Kid Power Agency.

297. Place, Marian T. **Boy Who Saw Bigfoot**. Dodd, Mead and Company, 1979.
95 p. ISBN: 0-396-07644-0; 0-396-08633-0 PB; GrL: 4-6; RdL: 2
Ten-year-old Joey Wilson lives with his new foster parents in western Washington. He tells the story of how he and his mother see the legendary Bigfoot. The reader learns various myths that have surrounded this creature. Joey and his classmates go on a field trip in the hopes of get a flimpse of Bigfoot.

298. Platt, Kin. **Ape Inside Me**. J.B. Lippincott, 1979.
117 p. ISBN: 0-397-31863-4 LB; 0-553-14825-7 PB; GrL: 6-up; RdL: 2
Kong, a voice inside 15-year-old Eddie Hill, screams "fight!"—constantly pushing him towards violence until he learns to channel this force into boxing.

299. Platt, Kin. **Brogg's Brain**. J.B. Lippincott, 1981.
123 p. ISBN: 0-397-31945-2; 0-397-31946-0 LB; GrL: 6-10; RdL: 2
Fifteen-year-old Monty Davis learns the power of positive thinking after seeing a strange science fiction movie and, with a little coaching from his new friend, drastically improves his running.

300. Platt, Kin. **Dracula, Go Home!** Franklin Watts/Dell, 1979/1981.
87 p. ISBN: 0-531-01464-9; 0-440-92022-1 PB; GrL: 4-6; RdL: 2; OP
Larry Carter is spending his summer helping out at his aunt's inn when he notices a suspicious guest who bears a ghastly resemblance to Dracula. This stranger never comes down to dinner, Larry observes him lurking in the cemetery, and the letters in his name (unscrambled) spell Dracula!

301. Platt, Kin. **Frank and Stein and Me**. Franklin Watts, 1982.
124 p. ISBN: 0-531-04169-7; GrL: 5-9; RdL: 2; OP
Jack goes to Paris when his sister, who won the trip, gets sick. From the start, he gets involved in a tangled web of crime and unusual characters when he unknowingly smuggles marijuana into France. The only person who helps him is the strange and vaguely familiar Dr. Stein.

302. Prelutsky, Jack. **What I Did Last Summer**. Greenwillow, 1984.
47 p. ISBN: 0-688-01754-1; 0-688-01755-X LB; GrL: 2-4; RdL: Varies
Collection of 13 humorous poems, told from a boy's point of view, of some of the things he did during summer vacation. These include accounts of his little brother losing his bathing suit at the beach, getting the flu in August and finally getting bored enough to want to return to school.

303. Quackenbush, Robert. **Piet Potter's First Case**. McGraw-Hill (A Piet Potter Mystery), 1980.
47 p. ISBN: 0-07-051021-0; GrL: 3-5; RdL: 3; OP
A young male sleuth solves cryptic messages to help neighbors find their million-dollar inheritance. Clues take them through the city in an exciting race against time. The puzzle is difficult to solve, but the fun lies in seeing the mystery solved.

304. Radin, Ruth Yaffe. **Tac's Island**. Macmillan, 1986.
74 p. ISBN: 0-02-775780-3; GrL: 4-6; RdL: 2
Ten-year-old Steve and his family are vacationing on an island off the coast of Virginia for a week. The first day he meets an unusual native, Tac, which stands for Thomas Andrew Carter. Despite their sometimes shaky relationship, the boys grow to become close friends.

305. Radlauer, Edward. **Motorcycle Mania**. Childrens Press (Ready, Get Set, Go), 1973.
32 p. ISBN: 0-516-07421-0; 0-516-47421-9 PB; GrL: 2-6; RdL: 1
Color photographs enhance a scant text on this very popular subject. There are only a few words on each page. Photographs show various types of motorcycles in action.

306. Renner, Beverly Hollett. **Hideaway Summer**. Harper & Row, 1978.
134 p. ISBN: 0-06-024862-9 TR: 0-06-024863-7 LB; GrL: 5-7; RdL: 4
Addie has been separated from her brother, Clay, since their parents split up. As they travel to their summer camp, they stop at their grandmother's farm to pay a brief visit, since she has died. They decide to hide there for the rest of the summer, and they learn about each other and surviving in the woods.

307. Rice, Earle. **Fear on Ice**. Fearon (SporTellers), 1981.
60 p. ISBN: 0-8224-6476-4 PB; GrL: 9-up; RdL: 4
Neal Calder, pro ice hockey player, learns to deal with violence on the ice.

308. Robinet, Harriette Gillem. **Ride the Red Cycle**.
Houghton Mifflin Company, 1980.
34 p. ISBN: 0-395-29183-6; GrL: 4-6; RdL: 4
Crippled after an early childhood illness, Jerome is confined to a wheelchair. But his determination and will to achieve are the themes of this moving story. He wants a tricycle. He gets one and practices. He succeeds in peddling it down the street and, to everyone's surprise, gets off and walks to his family.

309. Rockwell, Thomas. **How to Eat Fried Worms**. Franklin Watts/Dell, 1973/1975.
116 p. ISBN: 0-531-02631-0; 0-440-44545-0 PB; GrL: 3-6; RdL: 3
Alan bets $50 that his friend Billy cannot eat one worm daily for 15 days. Fast-paced, illustrated by Emily McCully, this story has a few surprises. The print could be larger, but the chapters are short and the subject intriguing to keep readers turning the pages.

310. Rockwell, Thomas. **How to Fight a Girl**. Franklin Watts, 1987.
112 p. ISBN: 0-531-10140-1 LB; 0-531-15082-8; GrL: 4-6; RdL: 3
In this sequel to How To Eat Fried Worms, Billy tries to save his new bike from Joe O'Hara and Alan Phelps who vow revenge. But their plan backfires when their secret weapon becomes Billy's friend instead.

311. Rodgers, Mary. **Freaky Friday**. Harper & Row, 1972.
145 p. ISBN: 06-025049-6; GrL: 4-7; RdL: 3
Comical plot unwinds when a rebellious daughter and her mother mysteriously exchange bodies for one day.

312. Roop, Peter. **Keep the Lights Burning, Abbie**. Carolrhoda Books, 1985.
40 p. ISBN: 0-87614-275-7; GrL: 3-6; RdL: 2
This exciting story tells of the brave Abbie Burgess and her family, who lived in a lighthouse off the coast of Maine in 1853. In the bitter cold of January, her father, the lighthouse keeper, went off for desperately needed supplies. Abbie was in charge of lighting the lamps in his absence.

313. Rosenbloom, Joseph. **Ridiculous Nicholas Riddle Book**. Sterling, 1981.
64 p. ISBN: 0-8069-4652-0; 0-8069-4653-9 LB; GrL: 2-6; RdL: Varies; OP
The text is composed of approximately 39 riddles that follow a boy through his daily activities from morning to night. They are simple and easily read with only one or two per page. The humor is appealing to middle graders: for example, "What color is a burp? Burple."

314. Rosenbloom, Joseph. **Spooky Riddles and Jokes**. Sterling, 1987.
128 p. ISBN: 0-8069-6576-2; 0-8069-6577-0 LB; GrL: 3-6; RdL: Varies
A collection of over 700 riddles and jokes of the supernatural realm including "School Spirit" and "This Is the End."

315. Rotsler, William. **Star Trek III: Short Stories**. Wanderer Books, 1984.
126 p. ISBN: 0-671-50139-9 PB; GrL: 6-up; RdL: 6
A collection of five stories based on the movie Star Trek III: The Search for Spock. It includes: "Azphari Enigma," "Vulcan, Klingon and an Angel," "Jungles of Memory," "World's End," and "As Old as Forever."

316. Roy, Ron. **Nightmare Island**. E.P. Dutton, 1981.
69 p. ISBN: 0-525-35905-2; GrL: 3-6; RdL: 3; OP
On their first solo camping trip to an island off the coast of Maine, Harley and his younger brother are trapped by a fire that begins mysteriously.

317. Roy, Ron. **What Has Ten Legs and Eats Corn Flakes?** Clarion, 1982.
48 p. ISBN: 0-89919-119-3; GrL: K-3; RdL: 2
An easy introduction on caring for hermit crabs, gerbils and chameleons as pets. Gives information about their habitats, eating habits and other needs.

318. Rylant, Cynthia. **Henry and Mudge in the Green Time**. Bradbury Press, 1987.
48 p. ISBN: 0-02-778003-1; GrL: 1-3; RdL: 1
Another adventure of Henry and his dog-pal as they go on a summertime picnic, take a bath in the garden, hike to the top of a big green hill and bask.

319. Rylant, Cynthia. **Henry and Mudge: The First Book**. Bradbury Press, 1987.
39 p. ISBN: 0-02-778001-5; GrL: 1-3; RdL: 1
Henry, an only child, feels lonely until his parents get him a dog. They share adventures together until one day Mudge gets lost. Warm stories of the good times shared by a boy and his dog.

320. Rylant, Cynthia. **Henry and Mudge: Under the Yellow Moon**. Bradbury Press, 1987.
48 p. ISBN: 0-02-778004-X; GrL: 1-3; RdL: 1
In the fall Henry and his companion dog, Mudge, watch the leaves turn colors, meet Halloween spooks and share Thanksgiving dinner.

321. Savitz, Harriet May. **Swimmer**. Scholastic, 1986.
89 p. ISBN: 0-590-33946-X PB; GrL: 4-6; RdL: 3
Skip, who lives alone with his mother, finds a stray dog swimming in the ocean. He befriends him and hides him in an abandoned house, hoping to keep him one day.

322. Schwartz, Alvin. **In a Dark, Dark Room and Other Scary Stories**. Harper & Row (I Can Read), 1984.
63 p. ISBN: 0-06025274-X LB; 0-06-444090-7 PB; GrL: K-3; RdL: 1
Seven scary yarns based on traditional stories and folktales from different countries, told in a very simple way.

323. Schwartz, Alvin. **Scary Stories to Tell in the Dark**. J.B. Lippincott, 1981.
128 p. ISBN: 0-397-31926-6; 0-397-31927-4 LB; GrL: 4-6; RdL: 3
Eerie tales, songs and legends from American folklore, including the grim and the kind that make you grin. They include traditional "jump" stories, which cause the listening audience to do just that. About 30 stories in all with notes, sources and bibliography appended.

324. Seuss, Dr. **Cat in the Hat Comes Back**. Random House (Beginner Books), 1958.
62 p. ISBN: 0-394-80002-8 TR; 0-394-90002-2 LB; GrL: 1-3; RdL: 1
The Cat in the Hat returns, playing tricks when he takes a bath that leaves a pink spot in the tub that cannot be easily removed. It slides to many other places before it is finally cleaned up by 26 other tiny cats.

325. Seuss, Dr. **Cat in the Hat**. Random House (Beginner Books), 1957.
61 p. ISBN: 0-394-80001-X; 0-394-90001-4 LB; GrL: 1-3; RdL: 1
Two children are stuck in the house on a rainy day and are bored until a cat wearing a tall hat shows up and turns dull into delightful but not without a big mess.

326. Sharmat, Marjorie Weinman. **Get Rich Mitch!** Morrow, 1985.
     152 p. ISBN: 0-688-05790-X; GrL: 4-6; RdL: 3
     Mitch (from the first book, Rich Mitch tells the story of his latest claim to
     fame. His mother has arranged the marketing of Rich Mitch look-alike
     dolls, much to Mitch's dismay. Mitch gets even richer, but not without com-
     plications. He gets bombarded by fans and eventually abducted.

327. Sharmat, Marjorie Weinman. **Getting Something on Maggie Marmelstein.**
     Harper & Row, 1971.
     101 p. ISBN: 06-440038-7; GrL: 3-6; RdL: 3
     In this sequel to Marjorie W. Maggie Marmelstein for President, Thad and
     Maggie are rivals in a tit-for-tat relationship. Each tries to embarrass the
     other in front of classmates to compete for their attention.

328. Sharmat, Marjorie Weinman. **Nate the Great and the Fishy Prize.** Coward,
     McCann and Geoghegan, 1985.
     47 p. ISBN: 0-698-30745-3; GrL: 2-4; RdL: 3
     Though it means Nate cannot get his dog ready for the pet show, he agrees
     to search for the missing contest prize.

329. Sharmat, Marjorie Weinman. **Nate the Great and the Snowy Trail.** Cow-
     ard, McCann and Geoghegan, 1982.
     47 p. ISBN: 0-698-30738-0; GrL: 2-4; RdL: 2
     Rosamond's birthday present for Nate suddenly disappears, so Nate is hot
     on the trail to unravel the mystery. Only problem is she won't tell him what
     he is looking for because it's a surprise.

330. Shaw, Diana. **Gone Hollywood.** Little, Brown, and Company, 1988.
     143 p. ISBN: 0-316-78343-9; GrL: 6-9; RdL: 3
     Carter Colborn, teen sleuth, tries to solve the mystery of the disappearance
     of a television actress while visiting her writer-director father in California.

331. Shaw, Evelyn. **Alligator.** Harper & Row (Science I Can Read), 1972.
     60 p. ISBN: 06-025556-0 TR; 06-025557-9 LB; GrL: 2-4; RdL: 2
     Life cycle, eating habits and means of protection of the southeastern United
     States alligator are given in this easy-to-read book.

332. Shura, Mary Francis. **Barkley Street Six-Pack.** Dodd, 1979.
     159 p. ISBN: 0-396-07714-5; GrL: 4-6; RdL: 4
     Jane is shy but delighted with her new best friend who appears to know
     magic. This new relationship causes her to lose her old neighborhood
     friends, but she finds comfort in a dog she finds in an abandoned house.

333. Silverstein, Shel. **Light in the Attic**. Harper & Row, 1981.
167 p. ISBN: 0-06-025673-7; 0-06-025674-5 LB; GrL: 1-6; RdL: Varies
This collection of extremely popular, clever, silly and serious rhymes covers topics that are near and dear to the reader's life experiences; for example, overdue library books, bratty siblings, nail-biters and nose-pickers. The book includes zany illustrations and an index. Companion book: Where the Sidewalk Ends.

334. Simon, Seymour. **Einstein Anderson, Science Sleuth**. Viking, 1980.
73 p. ISBN: 0-670-29069-6; GrL: 4-6; RdL: 3
Ten science puzzles challenge the reader along with Einstein in this first book of the series. Clues and background information are given, Einstein solves the mystery and the reader is invited to guess how he did it. The answers are given on the next page. A variety of topics is included.

335. Simon, Seymour. **Paper Airplane Book**. Puffin, 1987.
48 p. ISBN: 0-14-030-925-X PB; GrL: 3-6; RdL: 4
A variety of easy-to-fold airplanes are presented with clear instructions and illustrations.

336. Singer, Marilyn. **It Can't Hurt Forever**. Harper & Row, 1978.
186 p. ISBN: 0-06-025681-8; 0-06-025682-6 LB; GrL: 4-6; RdL: 3
Ellie Simon has a heart defect and tells about her hospital experience. She is afraid of an upcoming operation until she meets Sonia, a young patient who has had surgery, who helps her deal with her fears.

337. Skurzynski, Gloria. **Minstrel in the Tower**. Random House (Stepping Stone Books), 1988.
62 p. ISBN: 0-394-89598-3 PB; 0-394-99598-8 LB; GrL: 2-4; RdL: 2
In the year 1195 Roger and Alice lost their father during the Crusades. They search for their mother's long-lost brother to save their mother's life.

338. Slote, Alfred. **C.O.L.A.R.: A Tale of Outer Space**. J.B. Lippincott, 1981.
145 p. ISBN: 0-397-31936-3; 0-397-31937-1 LB; GrL: 4-6; RdL: 4
Stranded on an unknown planet when their spaceship runs out of fuel, Jack Jameson and his family must rely on his robot twin, Danny, to save their lives. This is a sequel to My Robot Buddy.

339. Slote, Alfred. **Friend Like That**. J.B. Lippincott, 1988.
152 p. ISBN: 0-397-32310-7; 0-397-32311-5 LB; GrL: 4-6; RdL: 3
This is a sequel to Moving In, in which 11-year-old Robby wants to run away from his problems. He has moved to a new house and now must get used to his father's new girlfriend. He wants to run away but thanks to a new friend, Beth, he learns to adjust.

340. Slote, Alfred. **Hotshot**. Franklin Watts, 1977.
87 p. ISBN: 0-531-00330-2; GrL: 3-6; RdL: 2; OP
Paddy O'Neill, an ice hockey player, wants to score a goal so badly that he
is willing to monopolize the puck, causing his team to lose. When he gets a
second chance in a big game, he faces his yearning once again. With black-
and-white photos.

341. Slote, Alfred. **Moving In**. J.B. Lippincott, 1988.
167 p. ISBN: 0-397-32261-5; 0-397-32262-3 LB; GrL: 4-6; RdL: 3
Eleven-year-old Robby Miller and his sister, Peggy, try various schemes to
sabotage their father's new romance. Robby comes up with a desperate plan
of his own that's illegal and does more harm than good.

342. Slote, Alfred. **My Trip to Alpha I**. J.B. Lippincott, 1978.
94 p. ISBN: 0-397-31810-3; GrL: 4-6; RdL: 4
Young Jack Stevenson tells the story of his trip six million light-years away
to visit his aunt on Alpha I. He travels by VOYA-CODE in a matter of sec-
onds. He arrives only to find out that a greedy couple has reprogrammed a
clone of his aunt to force her to surrender her extensive property to them.

343. Slote, Alfred. **Omega Station**. J.B. Lippincott, 1983.
147 p. ISBN: 0-397-32035-3 TR; 0-397-32036-1 LB; GrL: 3-6; RdL: 3
In this sequel to C.O.L.A.R., Jack Jameson and Danny, his robot twin, travel
to Omega Station to try and save the universe from the mad scientist Otto
Drago.

344. Smith, Alison. **Help! There's a Cat Washing in Here!** E.P. Dutton, 1981.
152 p. ISBN: 0-525-31630-2; GrL: 4-6; RdL: 4
Henry must take care of his brother and sister and all the housework when
his mother decides to go back to work. He realizes there's more to it than he
thought, but he still thinks it's better than having bossy Aunt Wilhemina
move in and take over.

345. Smith, Doris Buchanan. **Taste of Blackberries**. Thomas Y. Crowell, 1973.
58 p. ISBN: 0-690-80511-X; 0-690-80512-8 LB; GrL: 4-6; RdL: 4
A harmless prank ends in tragedy when Jamie gets stung by bees while he
and his friend pick blackberries.

346. Sobol, Donald J. **Encyclopedia Brown Boy Detective**. Elsevier/Nelson;
Bantam, 1963;1978.
88 p. ISBN: 0-525-67200-1; 0-553-15359-5 PB; GrL: 3-6; RdL: 3
This is the first of many in this popular series of the boy wonder whose
brain is like an encyclopedia. The famous cast of characters, including Bugs
Meany, presents mind-benders to this child-sleuth. Of course he solves
them, but not without giving his reader a chance to solve them first.

347. Sobol, Donald J. **Encyclopedia Brown's 3rd Record Book of Weird & Wonderful Facts**. Morrow, 1985.
134 p. ISBN: 0-688-05705-5; GrL: 3-8; RdL: Varies
This miscellany of delightful curiosities and lesser-known facts is grouped into six categories, including Gym Dandies, Aspirin Alley, and Finders Keepers? These facts range from antiquity through the 1980s and from all around the world. Comical illustrations by Sal Murdocca accentuate the tidbits.

348. Sommer-Bodenburg, Angela. **My Friend the Vampire**. E.P. Dutton, 1982.
155 p. ISBN: 0-8037-0045-8; 0-8037-0046-6 LB; GrL: 4-6; RdL: 3
The graveside adventures of nine-year-old Tony Noodleman and his newly found vampire friends, Rudolph and Anna the Toothless, are sure to delight readers. Tony is curled in bed one night reading a horror story when he meets the vampire. Rudolph becomes his best friend.

349. Sorrels, Roy. **New Life**. New Readers Press, 1982.
64 p. ISBN: 0-88336-708-4; GrL: 8-up; RdL: 3
Scott and Donna are skating in the woods when they discover an old man who has been wounded, in the snow. He directs them to a woman who is about to give birth and Donna must use her nursing skills with no doctor, during a blizzard.

350. Stevens, Carla. **Trouble for Lucy**. Clarion, 1979.
80 p. ISBN: 0-89919-523-7; GrL: 2-5; RdL: 3
The Stewart family heads west to Oregon by wagon train. They encounter friendly Indians, fearsome weather, especially when Finn's (young girl) frisky puppy gets lost in a storm. The story is based on authentic journals. History notes included.

351. Stevenson, Drew. **Case of the Wandering Werewolf**. Dodd, 1987.
128 p. ISBN: 0-396-09154-7; GrL: 4-6; RdL: 3
Raymond Almond and J. Huntley English try to track down a wolflike beast that haunts the woods. Sequel to The Case of the Horrible Swamp Monster.

352. Strasser, Todd. **Rock 'N' Roll Nights**. Dell (Laurel-Leaf), 1982.
217 p. ISBN: 0-440-97318-X; GrL: 7-up; RdL: 5
Gary's rock group is headed for the top. The band gets to play in a local club but this rise to the top is not without its pitfalls. And one of them is Gary's growing attraction to his first cousin, who plays bass in the group.

353. Sullivan, George. **Center**. Thomas Y. Crowell, 1988.
58 p. ISBN: 0-690-04580-8; 0-690-04582-4 LB; GrL: 6-9; RdL: 6
Explains techniques, skills, strategies and all that it takes to play the center position well in basketball. With black-and-white photographs and illustrations.

354. Sullivan, George. **Pitcher**. Thomas Y. Crowell, 1986.
53 p. ISBN: 0-690-04538-7; 0-690-04539-5; GrL: 3-6; RdL: 4
Author describes techniques for becoming a better pitcher. The book is clearly written, with black-and-white photos as well as humorous cartoons by Don Madden. It addresses both males and females in a conversational yet practical tone. Some knowledge of this sport is helpful.

355. Tapp, Kathy Kennedy. **Den 3 Meets the Jinx**. McElderry Books, 1988.
118 p. ISBN: 0-689-50453-5 LB; GrL: 3-5; RdL: 3
Adam is upset that his bratty younger sister, Jessie, may have ruined his entire year, especially when it comes to his Cub Scout Den. Surprisingly, his sister may be the only one who can save the den from breaking up.

356. Thomas, Jane Resh. **Comeback Dog**. Houghton Mifflin Company/Clarion Books, 1981.
62 p. ISBN: 0-395-29432-0; GrL: 4-6; RdL: 5
A boy is still grieving for the loss of his dog when he discovers another one that is barely alive. It looks as if it has been beaten and can scarcely breathe. He takes it to his farmhouse and nurses it back to health. Though the dog doesn't respond the way his old dog did, Daniel learns to accept her.

357. Thorne, Ian. **Frankenstein**. Crestwood House (Monsters), 1977.
46 p. ISBN: 0-913940-66-6 LB; 0-913940-73-9 PB; GrL: 2-6; RdL: 3
This extremely popular series is a balance of black-and-white movie stills, dialogue and text. The volume gives the background of Mary Shelley's novel, bringing the reader up to the latest interpretations of the thriller in the movies and on television.

358. Timmons, Stan. **Black Gold Conspiracy**. Fearon (Double Fastback Spy), 1988.
62 p. ISBN: 0-8224-2409-6 PB; GrL: 9-up; RdL: 4
Bestselling author David Cole is approached by a fan who asks his help because someone is trying to kill him. Cole turns him down, the man is murdered and now his own life is in jeopardy.

359. Tripp, Valerie. **Molly Saves the Day: A Summer Story**. Pleasant Company (American Girls), 1988.
69 p. ISBN: 0-937295-42-6; 0-937295-43-4 PB; GrL: 2-6; RdL: 3
Molly attends Camp Gowonagin with her friends in 1944. When the counselor announces a Color War she is afraid the fun will end when she and her friends are put on different teams. And she realizes her biggest fear that she'll have to swim under water in order to win the game.

360. Van Woerkom, Dorothy. **Becky and the Bear**. Putnam, 1975.
42 p. ISBN: 399-60924-5 LB; 399-20434-2 TR; GrL: 2-4; RdL: 2; OP
After a hard winter in Maine, Becky's father and brother go, leaving Becky home with dull household tasks. But she, too, wishes to do something brave. Her chance comes when she figures a clever way to single-handedly capture a bear who is after their pigs.

361. Vedral, Joyce L. **Opposite Sex Is Driving Me Crazy**. Ballantine, 1988.
192 p. ISBN: 0-345-35221-1 PB; GrL: 6-up; RdL: 5
A reassuring question-and-answer book of teenage concerns about dealing with the opposite sex. Discussion includes dating, love, sex, rejection and responses from teens themselves.

362. Viorst, Judith. **Tenth Good Thing About Barney**. Atheneum, 1971.
25 p. ISBN: 0-689-20688-7; 0-689-71203-0 PB; GrL: K-4; RdL: 2
A young boy tells about the death of his pet cat and how the family members grieve for him in a positive way.

363. Wagner, Jane. **J.T.** Dell, 1971.
124 p. ISBN: 0-440-44275-3 PB; GrL: 3-6; RdL: 4
Based on a television film, this is the moving story of inner-city boy who gets attached to an alley cat that he saves. The cat becomes an outlet for the love he cannot express to anyone else.

364. Wagner, Robin S. **Sarah T.: Portrait of a Teen-Age Alcoholic**. Ballantine, 1975.
120 p. ISBN: 0-345-34242-9; GrL: 7-up; RdL: 4
Based on a television drama in which a teenage girl, distraught over her mother's remarriage, new home and school, starts drinking alcohol to cope. She thinks she can handle it but learns too late that she would do anything for a drink—and she does.

365. Walker, Alice. **Langston Hughes, American Poet**. Crowell, 1974.
33 p. ISBN: 0-690-00218-1 TR; 0-690-00219-X LB; GrL: 3-6; RdL: 4
The story of Langston Hughes from his early life in Mexico to his return to the United States where he became a famous poet.

366. Wallace, Bill. **Danger on Panther Peak**. Simon & Schuster, 1985.
155 p. ISBN: 0-671-61282-4; GrL: 3-6; RdL: 2
During a blizzard, Tom must ride through panther territory to get help for his injured grandfather. To his amazement he confronts the panther in an encounter that could kill him.

367. Walter, Mildred Pitts. **Mariah Loves Rock**. Bradbury Press, 1988.
117 p. ISBN: 0-02-792511-0; GrL: 4-6; RdL: 3
The excitement of graduation and tickets to her idol's rock concert aren't enough to calm Mariah's fears about the arrival of her half-sister, Denise, who is moving in.

368. Weber, Bruce. **Bruce Weber's Inside Pro Football 1988**. Scholastic, 1988. 106 p. ISBN: 0-590-41728-2 PB; GrL: 6-up; RdL: 5
A look at major teams from the National Football League, including spotlights on key players of the 1988 season and statistics from the previous year.

369. White, Robb. **Deathwatch**. Dell, 1972. 220 p. ISBN: 0-440-91740-9 PB; GrL: 6-up; RdL: 4
Ben is left stripped in the desert by a cold-blooded hunter when an old prospector is accidently killed. Now it's a survival race against time and odds with deadly consequences.

370. Williams, Jan. **Danny Dunn, Scientific Detective**. Archway/Pocket Books, 1977. 172 p. ISBN: 0-671-44382-8 PB; GrL: 4-7; RdL: 3; OP
Science-fiction sleuth Danny and his pals, Joe and Irene, put their heads together to try and clear the accusations that their friend, Professor, is part of a robbery and kidnapping of the manager of a local department store. Danny invents Bleeper, a robot bloodhound that looks like a vacuum cleaner.

371. Wolkoff, Judie. **Wally**. Bradbury Press/Apple Paperbacks, 1977/1982. 199 p. ISBN: 0-87888-125-5; 0-590-32134-X PB; GrL: 4-6; RdL: 4
Funny account of two brothers who hide a chuckwalla (member of the lizard family) from the rest of their family. The story takes off when the chuckwalla does. It appears briefly in their sister's bedroom one night and then makes what turns out to be a very timely appearance during a visit by prospective house buyers.

372. Wright, Betty Ren. **Pike River**. Holiday House, 1988. 153 p. ISBN: 0-8234-0721-7; GrL: 7-up; RdL: 4
Thirteen-year-old Rachel and her friend, Charlie, meet a fierce ghost of an old lady who is eerily involved with an upcoming Sunbonnet Queen contest.

373. Yolen, Jane. **Commander Toad and the Space Pirates**. Coward-McCann, Inc.(Commander Toad), 1987. 62 p. ISBN: 0-698-20633-9 PB; 0-698-30749-6 LB; GrL: 2-4; RdL: 1
The latest offering in the Commander Toad series filled with fun and puns. Commander's ship, Star Warts, is captured by Commander Salamander and his band of pirates.

374. Yolen, Jane. **Robot and Rebecca: The Mystery of the Code-Carrying Kids**. Alfred A. Knopf (Capers), 1980. 89 p. ISBN: 0-394-84488-2; 0-394-94488-7 LB; GrL: 3-6; RdL: 4
This story is set in the year 2121 in an apartment-city where Rebecca lives. For her birthday, nine-year-old Rebecca gets a robot, which she programs to aid her in solving the mystery of the lost twins.

Title Index

Subject Index

Acceptance-Fiction
Blume, Judy. It's Not the End of the World; GrL: 5-8; RdL: 3

Blume, Judy. Tiger Eyes; GrL: 6-up; RdL: 3

Byars, Betsy. Good-bye, Chicken Little; GrL: 4-6; RdL: 4

Paulsen, Gary. Tracker; GrL: 6-up; RdL: 3

Walter, Mildred Pitts. Mariah Loves Rock; GrL: 4-6; RdL: 3

Accomplishment-Fiction
Mazer, Harry. War on Villa Street; GrL: 7-up; RdL: 5

Adoption
Krementz, Jill. How It Feels to Be Adopted; GrL: 3-up; RdL: Varies

Adventure
Avi. Man from the Sky; GrL: 4-6; RdL: 2

Bulla, Clyde Robert. Pirate's Promise; GrL: 3-6; RdL: 2

Clark, Margaret Goff. Barney and the UFO; GrL: 4-7; RdL: 4

Clifford, Eth. Help! I'm a Prisoner in the Library; GrL: 4-6; RdL: 2

Corbett, Scott. Great McGoniggle Rides Shotgun; GrL: 3-6; RdL: 2

Donnelly, Judy. True-Life Treasure Hunts; GrL: 4-6; RdL: 4

DuPrau, Jeanne. Golden God; GrL: 9-up; RdL: 5

Etrat, Jonathan. Aliens for Breakfast; GrL: 3-4; RdL: 3

Fife, Dale. Sesame Seed Snatchers; GrL: 4-6; RdL: 4

Girard, Ken. Double Exposure; GrL: 9-up; RdL: 5

Marzollo, Jean, and Claudio Marzollo. Jed and the Space Bandits; GrL: 1-3; RdL: 2

Mazer, Harry. Snow Bound; GrL: 6-up; RdL: 5

Milton, Hilary. Mayday! Mayday!; GrL: 6-up; RdL: 5

Morressy, John. Drought on Ziax II; GrL: 3-5; RdL: 3

Packard, Edward. Sunken Treasure; GrL: 4-6; RdL: 2

Paulsen, Gary. Hatchet; GrL: 8-up; RdL: 7

Place, Marian T. Boy Who Saw Bigfoot; GrL: 4-6; RdL: 2

Renner, Beverly Hollett. Hideaway Summer; GrL: 5-7; RdL: 4

Roy, Ron. Nightmare Island; GrL: 3-6; RdL: 3

Slote, Alfred. C.O.L.A.R.: A Tale of Outer Space; GrL: 4-6; RdL: 4

Slote, Alfred. My Trip to Alpha I; GrL: 4-6; RdL: 4

Slote, Alfred. Omega Station; GrL: 3-6; RdL: 3

Sorrels, Roy. New Life, A; GrL: 8-up; RdL: 3

Wallace, Bill. Danger on Panther Peak; GrL: 3-6; RdL: 2

White, Robb. Deathwatch; GrL: 6-up; RdL: 4

Afro-Americans-Biography
Adoff, Arnold. Malcolm X; GrL: 3-6; RdL: 3

Anderson, LaVere. Mary McLeod Bethune: Teacher with a Dream; GrL: 3-5; RdL: 3

Epstein, Sam, and Beryl Epstein. Harriet Tubman: Guide to Freedom; GrL: 4-6; RdL: 2

Walker, Alice. Langston Hughes, American Poet; GrL: 3-6; RdL: 4

Afro-Americans-Fiction
Bonham, Frank. Durango Street; GrL: 8-up; RdL: 6

Butterworth, W.E. LeRoy and the Old Man; GrL: 7-up; RdL: 3

Cameron, Ann. Julian's Glorious Summer; GrL: 1-3; RdL: 2

Cameron, Ann. Julian, Secret Agent;
    GrL: 1-3; RdL: 2
Myers, Walter Dean. Fallen Angels; GrL:
    9-up; RdL: 2
Myers, Walter Dean. Hoops; GrL: 7-up;
    RdL: 4
Wagner, Jane. J.T.; GrL: 3-6; RdL: 4
Walter, Mildred Pitts. Mariah Loves Rock;
    GrL: 4-6; RdL: 3

Airplanes
Petersen, David. Airplanes; GrL: 3-6;
    RdL: 3

Airplanes, Paper
Simon, Seymour. Paper Airplane Book;
    GrL: 3-6; RdL: 4

Alcohol-Fiction
Franklin, Lance. Takedown; GrL: 6-up;
    RdL: 4
Levy, Elizabeth. Dani Trap; GrL: 6-up;
    RdL: 3

Alcoholism-Fiction
Greene, Shep. Boy Who Drank Too
    Much; GrL: 6-up; RdL: 2
Mazer, Harry. War on Villa Street; GrL:
    7-up; RdL: 5
Wagner, Robin S. Sarah T.: Portrait of a
    Teen-Age Alcoholic; GrL: 7-up; RdL: 4

Alligators
Shaw, Evelyn. Alligator; GrL: 2-4;
    RdL: 2

American Revolution-Fiction
Moore, Allan. British Are Coming; GrL:
    9-up; RdL: 4

Animals
Eisler, Colin. Cats Know Best; GrL: P-3;
    RdL: 1
Glendinning, Sally. Doll: Bottle-Nosed
    Dolphin; GrL: 2-5; RdL: 3

Hart, Angela. Dogs; GrL: 2-6; RdL: 3
Patterson, Francine. Koko's Kitten; GrL:
    2-6; RdL: 3

Animals-Fiction
Berends, Polly. Case of the Elevator
    Duck; GrL: 4-6; RdL: 3
Cleary, Beverly. Socks; GrL: 4-6; RdL: 2
Hall, Lynn. Captain: Canada's Flying
    Pony; GrL: 3-6; RdL: 3
Hayward, Linda. Hello, House!; GrL: 1-
    3; RdL: 1
Kessler, Leonard. Old Turtle's Baseball
    Stories; GrL: 1-3;
    RdL: 1
Kessler, Leonard. Old Turtle's Riddle and
    Joke Book; GrL: 1-3; RdL: 1
King, P.E. Down on the Funny Farm;
    GrL: 1-3; RdL: 1
Thomas, Jane Resh. Comeback Dog;
    GrL: 4-6; RdL: 5
Wallace, Bill. Danger on Panther Peak;
    GrL: 3-6; RdL: 2

Archeologists-Fiction
DuPrau, Jeanne. Golden God; GrL: 9-up;
    RdL: 5

Archeology
Donnelly, Judy. Tut's Mummy: Lost..and
    Found; GrL: 3-4; RdL: 2

Architects-Fiction
Cowen, Eve. Catch the Sun; GrL: 9-up;
    RdL: 5

Arson-Fiction
Law, Carol Russell. Case of the Weird
    Street Firebug; GrL: 4-6; RdL: 3

Art
Ames, Lee J. Draw Fifty Monsters,
    Creeps, Superheroes, etc.; GrL: 4-up;
    RdL: no words

Artists-Fiction
Levoy, Myron. Shadow Like a Leopard, A; GrL: 6-up; RdL: 3

Astronauts-Biography
Blacknall, Carolyn. Sally Ride: America's First Woman in Space; GrL: 6-9; RdL: 6

Astronomy
Branley, Franklyn Mansfield. Eclipse: Darkness in Daytime; GrL: 1-4; RdL: 2

Autobiography
Anonymous. Go Ask Alice; GrL: 7-up; RdL: 4

Autumn-Fiction
Krensky, Stephen. Lionel in the Fall; GrL: 1-3; RdL: 2
Rylant, Cynthia. Henry and Mudge: Under the Yellow Moon; GrL: 1-3; RdL: 1

Babies
Brown, Fern G. Teen Guide to Childbirth; GrL: 6-up; RdL: 4

Babysitting-Fiction
Bates, Betty. Love Is Like Peanuts; GrL: 6-up; RdL: 3

Baking-Fiction
Gauch, Patricia Lee. Aaron and the Green Mountain Boys; GrL: 1-4; RdL: 2

Balloonists-Fiction
Bromley, Dudley. Balloon Spies; GrL: 7-up; RdL: 4

Baseball
Aaseng, Nathan. Baseball: It's Your Team; GrL: 6-up; RdL: 7
Appel, Marty. First Book of Baseball; GrL: 2-6; RdL: 4
Cluck, Bob. Baserunning; GrL: 6-9; RdL: 6
Cluck, Bob. Hitting; GrL: 6-9; RdL: 6

Cluck, Bob. Shortstop; GrL: 6-9; RdL: 6
Greene, Carol. I Can Be a Baseball Player; GrL: 1-4; RdL: 2
Kalb, Jonah. Easy Baseball Book; GrL: 2-5; RdL: 2
Sullivan, George. Pitcher; GrL: 3-6; RdL: 4

Baseball-Fiction
Christopher, Matt. Hit-Away Kid; GrL: 3-5; RdL: 3
Franklin, Lance. Double Play; GrL: 6-up; RdL: 5
Giff, Patricia Reilly. Ronald Morgan Goes to Bat; GrL: 3-4; RdL: 1
Harris, Robie H. Rosie's Double Dare; GrL: 3-6; RdL: 2
Kalb, Jonah. Goof That Won the Pennant; GrL: 3-6; RdL: 4
Kessler, Leonard. Old Turtle's Baseball Stories; GrL: 1-3; RdL: 1
Kline, Suzy. Herbie Jones and the Monster Ball; GrL: 3-5; RdL: 3
Landon, Lucinda. Meg Mackintosh and the Case of the Missing Babe Ruth Baseball; GrL: 2-4; RdL: 2
Levy, Elizabeth. Something Queer at the Ballpark; GrL: 2-4; RdL: 2
Lewis, Marjorie. Wrongway Applebaum; GrL: 4-6; RdL: 4
Park, Barbara. Skinnybones; GrL: 4-6; RdL: 4

Basketball
Sullivan, George. Center; GrL: 6-9; RdL: 6

Basketball-Fiction
Christopher, Matt. Red-Hot Hightops; GrL: 6-9; RdL: 3
Gutman, Bill. Smitty; GrL: 6-up; RdL: 4
Hallowell, Tommy. Out of Bounds; GrL: 6-up; RdL: 5
Myers, Walter Dean. Hoops; GrL: 7-up; RdL: 4
O'Connor, Dick. Foul Play; GrL: 9-up; RdL: 4

Bears-Fiction

Berenstain, Stan. Bike Lesson; GrL: P-3;
RdL: 1

Behavior-Fiction

Christopher, Matt. Hit-Away Kid; GrL: 3-
5; RdL: 3

Bethune, Mary McLeod. Anderson, LaVere.
Mary McLeod Bethune: Teacher with a
Dream; GrL: 3-5; RdL: 3

Bicycles-Fiction

Berenstain, Stan. Bike Lesson; GrL: P-3;
RdL: 1

Cameron, Ann. Julian's Glorious
Summer; GrL: 1-3; RdL: 2

Biography

Adams, Barbara Johnston. Picture Life of
Bill Cosby; GrL: 4-6; RdL: 3

Adoff, Arnold. Malcolm X; GrL: 3-6;
RdL: 3

Anderson, LaVere. Mary McLeod
Bethune: Teacher with a Dream; GrL:
3-5; RdL: 3

Blacknall, Carolyn. Sally Ride: America's
First Woman in Space; GrL: 6-9;
RdL: 6

Blinn, William. Brian's Song; GrL: 6-up;
RdL: 2

Brown, Drollene P. Sybil Rides for
Independence; GrL: 4-6; RdL: 4

Colver, Anne. Abraham Lincoln; GrL: 4-
6; RdL: 2

Davidson, Margaret. Story of Benjamin
Franklin, Amazing American; GrL: 4-
6; RdL: 3

Edwards, Anne. Great Houdini; GrL: 4-6;
RdL: 3

Eichhorn, Dennis P. Springsteen; GrL: 6-
up; RdL: 4

Epstein, Sam, and Beryl Epstein. Harriet
Tubman: Guide to Freedom; GrL: 4-6;
RdL: 2

Franchere, Ruth. Cesar Chavez; GrL: 4-6;
RdL: 3

Goodsell, Jane. Eleanor Roosevelt; GrL:
2-4; RdL: 2

Heilbroner, Joan. Meet George
Washington; GrL: 4-6; RdL: 2

Latham, Jean Lee. Elizabeth Blackwell:
Pioneer Woman Doctor; GrL: 3-6; RdL: 3

Levine, Ellen. Secret Missions: Four True
Life Stories; GrL: 3-6; RdL: 4

Malone, Mary. Annie Sullivan; GrL: 2-4;
RdL: 3

Roop, Peter. Keep the Lights Burning,
Abbie; GrL: 3-6; RdL: 2

Walker, Alice. Langston Hughes,
American Poet; GrL: 3-6; RdL: 4

Birth Control

Nourse, Alan E. Teen Guide to Birth
Control; GrL: 6-up;
RdL: 6

Blackwell, Elizabeth

Latham, Jean Lee. Elizabeth Blackwell:
Pioneer Woman Doctor; GrL: 3-6;
RdL: 3

Brothers and Sisters-Fiction

Adler, C.S. Split Sisters; GrL: 5-up;
RdL: 5

Byars, Betsy. Golly Sisters Go West;
GrL: K-3; RdL: 1

Byars, Betsy. Summer of the Swans;
GrL: 6-9; RdL: 6

Mazer, Harry. When the Phone Rang;
GrL: 6-up; RdL: 3

Pevsner, Stella. Sister of the Quints; GrL:
6-9; RdL: 2

Renner, Beverly Hollett. Hideaway
Summer; GrL: 5-7; RdL: 4

Skurzynski, Gloria. Minstrel in the Tower;
GrL: 2-4; RdL: 2

Tapp, Kathy Kennedy. Den 3 Meets the
Jinx; GrL: 3-5; RdL: 3

Camping

Gray, William R. Camping Adventure;
GrL: 3-6; RdL: 2

Camping-Fiction
Boutis, Victoria. Katy Did It; GrL: 4-6;
RdL: 3

Camps-Fiction
Roy, Ron. Nightmare Island; GrL: 3-6;
RdL: 3
Cole, Brock. Goats; GrL: 6-up; RdL: 2
O'Connor, Jim, and Jane O'Connor. Ghost
in Tent 19; GrL: 4-6; RdL: 3
Tripp, Valerie. Molly Saves the Day: A
Summer Story; GrL: 2-6; RdL: 3

Car Accidents-Fiction
Bunting, Eve. Ghosts of Departure Point;
GrL: 5-up; RdL: 2
Duncan, Lois. I Know What You Did Last
Summer; GrL: 7-up; RdL: 3

Car Racing
Barrett, Norman S. Racing Cars; GrL: 3-
6; RdL: 4

Careers-Fiction
Haas, Dorothy. To Catch a Crook; GrL:
4-6; RdL: 3

Cats
Eisler, Colin. Cats Know Best; GrL: P-3;
RdL: 1
Kuklin, Susan. Taking My Cat to the Vet;
GrL: K-3; RdL: 2

Cats-Fiction
Cleary, Beverly. Socks; GrL: 4-6; RdL: 2
Giff, Patricia Reilly. Powder Puff Puzzle;
GrL: 2-4; RdL: 1
Hooks, William H. Pioneer Cat; GrL: 3-
4; RdL: 2
Orgel, Doris. Whiskers Once and Always;
GrL: 3-5; RdL: 2
Seuss, Dr. Cat in the Hat Comes Back;
GrL: 1-3; RdL: 1
Viorst, Judith. Tenth Good Thing About
Barney; GrL: K-4; RdL: 2
Wagner, Jane. J.T.; GrL: 3-6; RdL: 4

Cats-Poetry
Larrick, Nancy. Cats Are Cats; GrL: All
ages; RdL: Varies

Cave Men-Fiction
Hoff, Syd. Stanley; GrL: 1-3; RdL: 2

Celebrities-Fiction
Martin, Ann M. Just a Summer Romance;
GrL: 6-9; RdL: 3
Miles, Betty. Secret Life of the Underwear
Champ; GrL: 3-5; RdL: 2
Sharmat, Marjorie Weinman. Get Rich
Mitch!; GrL: 4-6;
RdL: 3
Chavez, Cesar. Franchere, Ruth. Cesar
Chavez; GrL: 4-6; RdL: 3

Cheating-Fiction
Marzollo, Jean. Red Ribbon Rosie; GrL:
2-4; RdL: 3

Childbirth
Brown, Fern G. Teen Guide to Childbirth;
GrL: 6-up; RdL: 4

Chinese Americans-Fiction
Claypool, Jane. Jasmine Finds Love;
GrL: 6-up; RdL: 3

Codes and Ciphers
Peterson, John. How to Write Codes and
Send Secret Messages; GrL: 3-5;
RdL: 2

Collective Biography
Levine, Ellen. Secret Missions: Four True
Life Stories; GrL: 3-6; RdL: 4

Comedians-Fiction
Conford, Ellen. Strictly for Laughs; GrL:
6-up; RdL: 4

Competition-Fiction
Cowen, Eve. High Escape; GrL: 9-up;
RdL: 4

Cosby, Bill
Adams, Barbara Johnston. Picture Life of
Bill Cosby; GrL: 4-6; RdL: 3

Courage-Fiction
Fife, Dale. North of Danger; GrL: 5-9;
RdL: 4
Gauch, Patricia Lee. Thunder at
Gettysburg; GrL: 4-6; RdL: 4
Milton, Hilary. Mayday! Mayday!; GrL:
6-up; RdL: 5

Crafts
Lopshire, Robert. How to Make Snop
Snappers and Other Fine Things; GrL:
K-4; RdL: 1

Crime
Madison, Arnold. Great Unsolved Cases;
GrL: 6-up; RdL: 3

Crime-Fiction
Platt, Kin. Frank and Stein and Me; GrL:
5-9; RdL: 2

Daisy Rothschild Giraffe
Leslie-Melville, Betty. Daisy Rothschild
Giraffe That Lives with Me; GrL: 4-8;
RdL: 6

Danish Tales
Bason, Lillian. Those Foolish Molboes;
GrL: 3-5; RdL: 3

Dares-Fiction
Harris, Robie H. Rosie's Double Dare;
GrL: 3-6; RdL: 2

Dating
Vedral, Joyce L. Opposite Sex Is Driving
Me Crazy; GrL: 6-up; RdL: 5

Dating-Fiction
Bunting, Eve. Janet Hamm Needs a Date
for the Dance; GrL: 6-9; RdL: 3

Deafness-Fiction
Montgomery, Elizabeth R. Mystery of the
Boy Next Door; GrL: 2-4; RdL: 1

Death
Krementz, Jill. How It Feels When a
Parent Dies; GrL: 3-up; RdL: Varies
Patterson, Francine. Koko's Kitten; GrL:
2-6; RdL: 3

Death-Fiction
Bauer, Marion Dane. On My Honor; GrL:
5-9; RdL: 3
Blume, Judy. Tiger Eyes; GrL: 6-up;
RdL: 3
Byars, Betsy. Good-bye, Chicken Little;
GrL: 4-6; RdL: 4
Mazer, Harry. When the Phone Rang;
GrL: 6-up; RdL: 3
Orgel, Doris. Whiskers Once and Always;
GrL: 3-5; RdL: 2
Paulsen, Gary. Tracker; GrL: 6-up;
RdL: 3
Pevsner, Stella. And You Give Me a Pain,
Elaine; GrL: 4-6; RdL: 3
Smith, Doris Buchanan. Taste of
Blackberries, A; GrL: 4-6; RdL: 4
Thomas, Jane Resh. Comeback Dog;
GrL: 4-6; RdL: 5
Viorst, Judith. Tenth Good Thing About
Barney; GrL: K-4; RdL: 2

Decision Making-Fiction
Franklin, Lance. Double Play; GrL: 6-up;
RdL: 5

Detectives-Fiction
Adler, David A. Cam Jansen & the
Mystery of the Stolen Diamonds; GrL:
2-4; RdL: 2
Fife, Dale. Follow That Ghost; GrL: 2-4;
RdL: 2
Fleischman, Paul. Phoebe Danger,
Detective in the Case of the Two-
Minute Cough; GrL: 4-5; RdL: 3

Fleischman, Sid. Bloodhound Gang in the Case of the Secret Message; GrL: 4-6; RdL: 4

Giff, Patricia Reilly. Have You Seen Hyacinth Macaw?; GrL: 4-6; RdL: 3

Howe, James. Stage Fright; GrL: 6-up; RdL: 4

Law, Carol Russell. Case of the Weird Street Firebug; GrL: 4-6; RdL: 3

Sharmat, Marjorie Weinman. Nate the Great and the Fishy Prize; GrL: 2-4; RdL: 3

Sharmat, Marjorie Weinman. Nate the Great and the Snowy Trail; GrL: 2-4; RdL: 2

Determination-Fiction

Cowen, Eve. Catch the Sun; GrL: 9-up; RdL: 5

Dinosaurs-Fiction

Adler, David A. Dinosaur Princess and Other Prehistoric Riddles; GrL: 2-5; RdL: 2

Hoff, Syd. Stanley; GrL: 1-3; RdL: 2

Disabled Children-Fiction

Montgomery, Elizabeth R. Mystery of the Boy Next Door; GrL: 2-4; RdL: 1

Robinet, Harriette Gillem. Ride the Red Cycle; GrL: 4-6; RdL: 4

Disc Jockeys-Fiction

Conford, Ellen. Strictly for Laughs; GrL: 6-up; RdL: 4

Disobedience-Fiction

Bauer, Marion Dane. On My Honor; GrL: 5-9; RdL: 3

Divorce

Krementz, Jill. How It Feels When Parents Divorce; GrL: 3-up; RdL: varies

Divorce-Fiction

Blume, Judy. It's Not the End of the World; GrL: 5-8; RdL: 3

Cleary, Beverly. Dear Mr. Henshaw; GrL: 5-8; RdL: 5

Park, Barbara. Don't Make Me Smile; GrL: 4-6; RdL: 3

Paulsen, Gary. Hatchet; GrL: 8-up; RdL: 7

Dogs

Bare, Colleen Stanley. To Love a Dog; GrL: 2-4; RdL: 2

Cole, Joanna. My Puppy Is Born; GrL: 1-4; RdL: 2

Hallum, Red. Kookie Rides Again; GrL: 2-6; RdL: 4

Hart, Angela. Dogs; GrL: 2-6; RdL: 3

Dogs-Fiction

Arnosky, Jim. Gray Boy; GrL: 6-8; RdL: 5

Rylant, Cynthia. Henry and Mudge in the Green Time; GrL: 1-3; RdL: 1

Rylant, Cynthia. Henry and Mudge: The First Book; GrL: 1-3; RdL: 1

Rylant, Cynthia. Henry and Mudge: Under the Yellow Moon; GrL: 1-3; RdL: 1

Savitz, Harriet May. Swimmer; GrL: 4-6; RdL: 3

Shura, Mary Francis. Barkley Street Six-Pack; GrL: 4-6; RdL: 4

Thomas, Jane Resh. Comeback Dog; GrL: 4-6; RdL: 5

Dolphins

Glendinning, Sally. Doll: Bottle-Nosed Dolphin; GrL: 2-5; RdL: 3

Drawing

Ames, Lee J. Draw Fifty Monsters, Creeps, Superheroes, etc.; GrL: 4-up; RdL: no words

Drawing-Fiction

Bulla, Clyde Robert. Chalk Box Kid; GrL: 2-4; RdL: 2

Drugs-Fiction

Anonymous. Go Ask Alice; GrL: 7-up; RdL: 4

Christopher, Matt. Tackle without a Team; GrL: 6-9; RdL: 2

Hinton, S.E. That Was Then, This Is Now; GrL: 7-12; RdL: 6

Eclipses

Branley, Franklyn Mansfield. Eclipse: Darkness in Daytime; GrL: 1-4; RdL: 2

Egypt-Excavations

Donnelly, Judy. Tut's Mummy: Lost..and Found; GrL: 3-4; RdL: 2

Employment-Fiction

Pfeffer, Susan Beth. Kid Power; GrL: 4-6; RdL: 4

Entertainers-Biography

Adams, Barbara Johnston. Picture Life of Bill Cosby; GrL: 4-6; RdL: 3

Enthusiasm-Fiction

Giff, Patricia Reilly. Ronald Morgan Goes to Bat; GrL: 3-4; RdL: 1

ESP-Fiction

Conford, Ellen. And This Is Laura; GrL: 4-7; RdL: 4

Kibbe, Pat. Hocus-Pocus Dilemma; GrL: 4-6; RdL: 4

Espionage-Fiction

Greene, Janice. Flight of the Sparrow; GrL: 9-up; RdL: 4

Experiments

Markle, Sandra. Science Mini-Mysteries; GrL: 4-6; RdL: Varies

Eyeglasses-Fiction

Giff, Patricia Reilly. Watch Out, Ronald Morgan; GrL: 1-3; RdL: 1

Fame-Fiction

Clifford, Eth. I Never Wanted to Be Famous; GrL: 4-6; RdL: 4

Family Life

Krementz, Jill. How It Feels to Be Adopted; GrL: 3-up; RdL: Varies

Krementz, Jill. How It Feels When a Parent Dies; GrL: 3-up; RdL: Varies

Krementz, Jill. How It Feels When Parents Divorce; GrL: 3-up; RdL: varies

Family Life-Fiction

Blume, Judy. It's Not the End of the World; GrL: 5-8; RdL: 3

Blume, Judy. Tales of a Fourth Grade Nothing; GrL: 3-6; RdL: 3

Bulla, Clyde Robert. Pirate's Promise; GrL: 3-6; RdL: 2

Byars, Betsy. Beans on the Roof; GrL: 2-4; RdL: 2

Byars, Betsy. Summer of the Swans; GrL: 6-9; RdL: 6

Cameron, Ann. More Stories Julian Tells; GrL: 2-4; RdL: 3

Cameron, Ann. Stories Julian Tells; GrL: 2-4; RdL: 3

Chaikin, Miriam. Aviva's Piano; GrL: 3-4; RdL: 3

Conford, Ellen. And This Is Laura; GrL: 4-7; RdL: 4

Conford, Ellen. Job for Jenny Archer; GrL: 2-4; RdL: 3

Danziger, Paula. Cat Ate My Gymsuit; GrL: 6-9; RdL: 5

Delton, Judy. Only Jody; GrL: 4-6; RdL: 3

Greenwald, Sheila. Valentine Rosy; GrL: 3-5; RdL: 3

Hall, Lynn. If Winter Comes; GrL: 6-up; RdL: 5

Harris, Robie H. Rosie's Double Dare; GrL: 3-6; RdL: 2

Hurwitz, Johanna. Aldo Applesauce; GrL: 3-5; RdL: 3

Kibbe, Pat. Hocus-Pocus Dilemma; GrL: 4-6; RdL: 4

Lewis, Marjorie. Wrongway Applebaum; GrL: 4-6; RdL: 4

Football. Berger, Melvin. Photo Dictionary of Football; GrL: 6-12; RdL: 5

Broekel, Ray. Football; GrL: 3-6; RdL: 2

Burchard, Marshall. Terry Bradshaw; GrL: 3-6; RdL: 4

Dolan, Edward F. Great Moments in the Super Bowl; GrL: 4-8; RdL: 3

Gutman, Bill. Pro Football's Record Breakers; GrL: 6-up; RdL: 6

Madden, John. First Book of Football; GrL: 6-up; RdL: 4

Weber, Bruce. Bruce Weber's Inside Pro Football 1988; GrL: 6-up; RdL: 5

Football-Biography

Blinn, William. Brian's Song; GrL: 6-up; RdL: 2

Football-Fiction

Christopher, Matt. Tackle without a Team; GrL: 6-9; RdL: 2

Foley, Louise Munro. Tackle 22; GrL: 2-4; RdL: 2

Foster Parents-Fiction

Place, Marian T. Boy Who Saw Bigfoot; GrL: 4-6; RdL: 2

Franklin, Benjamin

Davidson, Margaret. Story of Benjamin Franklin, Amazing American; GrL: 4-6; RdL: 3

Friendship-Fiction

Bunting, Eve. Girl in the Painting; GrL: 6-up; RdL: 5

Bunting, Eve. Janet Hamm Needs a Date for the Dance; GrL: 6-9; RdL: 3

Bunting, Eve. Karen Kepplewhite Is the World's Best Kisser; GrL: 4-6; RdL: 2

Bunting, Eve. Skateboard Four; GrL: 4-7; RdL: 3

Byars, Betsy. Burning Questions of Bingo Brown; GrL: 5-up; RdL: 5

Byars, Betsy. Good-bye, Chicken Little; GrL: 4-6; RdL: 4

Cameron, Ann. Julian, Secret Agent; GrL: 1-3; RdL: 2

Cameron, Ann. More Stories Julian Tells; GrL: 2-4; RdL: 3

Cameron, Ann. Stories Julian Tells; GrL: 2-4; RdL: 3

Cole, Joanna. Missing Tooth; GrL: 1-3; RdL: 1

DeClements, Barthe. Nothing's Fair in Fifth Grade; GrL: 4-6; RdL: 3

Giff, Patricia Reilly. Say "Cheese"; GrL: 4-6; RdL: 2

Greene, Carol. Jenny Summer; GrL: 2-4; RdL: 2

Heide, Florence Parry. Banana Twist; GrL: 4-6; RdL: 4

Hinton, S.E. That Was Then, This Is Now; GrL: 7-12; RdL: 6

Hurwitz, Johanna. Aldo Applesauce; GrL: 3-5; RdL: 3

Kline, Suzy. Herbie Jones; GrL: 3-4; RdL: 3

Lobel, Arnold. Frog and Toad Together; GrL: K-3; RdL: 1

Marzollo, Jean. Red Ribbon Rosie; GrL: 2-4; RdL: 3

Park, Barbara. Don't Make Me Smile; GrL: 4-6; RdL: 3

Radin, Ruth Yaffe. Tac's Island; GrL: 4-6; RdL: 2

Rockwell, Thomas. How to Eat Fried Worms; GrL: 3-6; RdL: 3

Rockwell, Thomas. How to Fight a Girl; GrL: 4-6; RdL: 3

Rylant, Cynthia. Henry and Mudge: Under the Yellow Moon; GrL: 1-3; RdL: 1

Sharmat, Marjorie Weinman. Getting Something on Maggie Marmelstein; GrL: 3-6; RdL: 3

Shura, Mary Francis. Barkley Street Six-Pack; GrL: 4-6; RdL: 4

Singer, Marilyn. It Can't Hurt Forever; GrL: 4-6; RdL: 3

Slote, Alfred. Friend Like That, A; GrL: 4-6; RdL: 3

Smith, Doris Buchanan. Taste of Blackberries, A; GrL: 4-6; RdL: 4

Frontier Life–United States.-Fiction
Hooks, William H. Pioneer Cat; GrL: 3-4; RdL: 2

Gambling-Fiction
Bennett, Jay. Skeleton Man; GrL: 7-up; RdL: 2

Games
Lopshire, Robert. How to Make Snop Snappers and Other Fine Things; GrL: K-4; RdL: 1

Gangs-Fiction
Bonham, Frank. Durango Street; GrL: 8-up; RdL: 6
Bunting, Eve. Someone Is Hiding on Alcatraz Island; GrL: 6-up; RdL: 3
Butterworth, W.E. LeRoy and the Old Man; GrL: 7-up; RdL: 3
Levoy, Myron. Shadow Like a Leopard, A; GrL: 6-up; RdL: 3

Ghosts
Dolan, Edward F. Great Mysteries of the Air; GrL: 4-6; RdL: 4

Ghosts-Fiction
Abels, Harriet Sheffer. Haunted Motorcycle Shop; GrL: 5-8; RdL: 3
Adler, David A. Jeffrey's Ghost and the Fifth-Grade Dragon; GrL: 3-5; RdL: 2
Avi. Devil's Race; GrL: 6-up; RdL: 2
Bunting, Eve. Ghosts of Departure Point; GrL: 5-up; RdL: 2
Carlson, Natalie Savage. Ghost in the Lagoon; GrL: 2-4; RdL: 2
Cohen, Daniel. Headless Roommate and Other Tales of Terror; GrL: 7-up; RdL: 5
Cohen, Daniel. Restless Dead; GrL: 4-up; RdL: 4
Eisenberg, Lisa, and Katy Hall. 101 Ghost Jokes; GrL: 4-up; RdL: 2
O'Connor, Jim, and Jane O'Connor. Ghost in Tent 19; GrL: 4-6; RdL: 3

Schwartz, Alvin. In a Dark, Dark Room and Other Scary Stories; GrL: K-3; RdL: 1
Schwartz, Alvin. Scary Stories to Tell in the Dark; GrL: 4-6; RdL: 3
Wright, Betty Ren. Pike River; GrL: 7-up; RdL: 4

Gifts-Fiction
Kline, Suzy. Herbie Jones and the Class Gift; GrL: 3-5; RdL: 3

Giraffes
Leslie-Melville, Betty. Daisy Rothschild Giraffe That Lives with Me; GrL: 4-8; RdL: 6

Grief-Fiction
Mazer, Harry. When the Phone Rang; GrL: 6-up; RdL: 3

Growing up-Fiction
Adler, C.S. Split Sisters; GrL: 5-up; RdL: 5
Arnosky, Jim. Gray Boy; GrL: 6-8; RdL: 5
Boutis, Victoria. Katy Did It; GrL: 4-6; RdL: 3
Davis, Jenny. Sex Education; GrL: 7-9; RdL: 2
Greenwald, Sheila. Valentine Rosy; GrL: 3-5; RdL: 3

Halloween-Fiction
Krensky, Stephen. Lionel in the Fall; GrL: 1-3; RdL: 2
Manes, Stephen. Hooples' Haunted House; GrL: 4-6; RdL: 3

Health
Brown, Fern G. Teen Guide to Childbirth; GrL: 6-up; RdL: 4
Cole, Joanna. Asking about Sex and Growing Up; GrL: 5-up; RdL: Varies
Nourse, Alan E. Teen Guide to Birth Control; GrL: 6-up; RdL: 6
Nourse, Alan E. Teen Guide to Safe Sex; GrL: 6-up; RdL: 6

Heart Surgery-Fiction
Singer, Marilyn. It Can't Hurt Forever;
GrL: 4-6; RdL: 3

Heroes-Fiction
Clifford, Eth. I Never Wanted to Be
Famous; GrL: 4-6; RdL: 4

Hiking-Fiction
Boutis, Victoria. Katy Did It; GrL: 4-6;
RdL: 3

Historical Fiction
Avi. Devil's Race; GrL: 6-up; RdL: 2
Benchley, Nathaniel. Sam the Minuteman;
GrL: 1-4; RdL: 2
Fife, Dale. North of Danger; GrL: 5-9;
RdL: 4
Gauch, Patricia Lee. Aaron and the Green
Mountain Boys; GrL: 1-4; RdL: 2
Gauch, Patricia Lee. Thunder at
Gettysburg; GrL: 4-6; RdL: 4
Monjo, Ferdinand N. Vicksburg Veteran;
GrL: 3-6; RdL: 2
Moore, Allan. British Are Coming; GrL:
9-up; RdL: 4
Myers, Walter Dean. Fallen Angels; GrL:
9-up; RdL: 2
Skurzynski, Gloria. Minstrel in the Tower;
GrL: 2-4; RdL: 2
Stevens, Carla. Trouble for Lucy; GrL: 2-
5; RdL: 3
Tripp, Valerie. Molly Saves the Day: A
Summer Story; GrL: 2-6; RdL: 3
Van Woerkom, Dorothy. Becky and the
Bear; GrL: 2-4; RdL: 2

History
Davidson, Margaret. Story of Benjamin
Franklin, Amazing American; GrL: 4-
6; RdL: 3
Donnelly, Judy. Titanic Lost and Found;
GrL: 2-4; RdL: 2
Donnelly, Judy. Who Shot the President?
The Death of John F. Kennedy; GrL: 3-
6; RdL: 4
Goodsell, Jane. Eleanor Roosevelt; GrL:
2-4; RdL: 2

Hobbies
Ames, Lee J. Draw Fifty Monsters,
Creeps, Superheroes, etc.; GrL: 4-up;
RdL: no words
Kalb, Jonah. Easy Baseball Book; GrL:
2-5; RdL: 2
Kalb, Jonah. Easy Hockey Book; GrL: 2-
5; RdL: 2
Kalb, Jonah. Easy Ice Skating Book;
GrL: 2-5; RdL: 2

Hockey
Kalb, Jonah. Easy Hockey Book; GrL: 2-
5; RdL: 2

Hockey-Fiction
Greene, Shep. Boy Who Drank Too
Much; GrL: 6-up; RdL: 2

Holocaust-Fiction
Arrick, Fran. Chernowitz!; GrL: 6-up;
RdL: 5

Honesty-Fiction
Bunting, Eve. Janet Hamm Needs a Date
for the Dance; GrL: 6-9; RdL: 3

Hope-Fiction
Luenn, Nancy. Unicorn Crossing; GrL: 3-
5; RdL: 3

Horror
Cohen, Daniel. Headless Roommate and
Other Tales of Terror; GrL: 7-up;
RdL: 5
Cohen, Daniel. Restless Dead; GrL: 4-up;
RdL: 4
DeWeese, Gene. Nightmares from Space;
GrL: 6-12; RdL: 2

Horses-Fiction
Cavanna, Betty. Banner Year; GrL: 7-up;
RdL: 4
Hall, Lynn. Captain: Canada's Flying
Pony; GrL: 3-6; RdL: 3
Hinton, S.E. Taming the Star Runner;
GrL: 7-up; RdL: 6

Hoff, Syd. Horse in Harry's Room; GrL: 1-4; RdL: 1

Hospitals-Fiction

Singer, Marilyn. It Can't Hurt Forever; GrL: 4-6; RdL: 3

Houdini, Harry

Edwards, Anne. Great Houdini; GrL: 4-6; RdL: 3

Housework-Fiction

Smith, Alison. Help! There's a Cat Washing in Here!; GrL: 4-6; RdL: 4

Hughes, Langston

Walker, Alice. Langston Hughes, American Poet; GrL: 3-6; RdL: 4

Humor

Adler, David A. Dinosaur Princess and Other Prehistoric Riddles; GrL: 2-5; RdL: 2

Adler, David A. Fourth Floor Twins and the Sand Castle Contest; GrL: 2-4; RdL: 2

Adler, David A. Jeffrey's Ghost and the Fifth-Grade Dragon; GrL: 3-5; RdL: 2

Angell, Judie. Dear Lola or How to Build Your Own Family; GrL: 4-6; RdL: 4

Avi. Romeo and Juliet: Together (and Alive) at Last; GrL: 5-8; RdL: 2

Berends, Polly. Case of the Elevator Duck; GrL: 4-6; RdL: 3

Berenstain, Stan. Bike Lesson; GrL: P-3; RdL: 1

Blume, Judy. Freckle Juice; GrL: 2-4; RdL: 3

Blume, Judy. Tales of a Fourth Grade Nothing; GrL: 3-6; RdL: 3

Byars, Betsy. Burning Questions of Bingo Brown; GrL: 5-up; RdL: 5

Byars, Betsy. Golly Sisters Go West; GrL: K-3; RdL: 1

Cameron, Ann. More Stories Julian Tells; GrL: 2-4; RdL: 3

Cameron, Ann. Stories Julian Tells; GrL: 2-4; RdL: 3

Cleary, Beverly. Socks; GrL: 4-6; RdL: 2

Clifford, Eth. I Never Wanted to Be Famous; GrL: 4-6; RdL: 4

Conford, Ellen. If This Is Love, I'll Take Spaghetti; GrL: 6-up; RdL: 4

Conford, Ellen. Job for Jenny Archer; GrL: 2-4; RdL: 3

Conford, Ellen. Things I Did for Love; GrL: 6-up; RdL: 4

Corbett, Scott. Great McGoniggle Rides Shotgun; GrL: 3-6; RdL: 2

Cynthia, Blair. Marshmallow Masquerade; GrL: 6-up; RdL: 4

Delton, Judy. Only Jody; GrL: 4-6; RdL: 3

Dubowski, Cathy East. Pretty Good Magic; GrL: 1-3; RdL: 2

Eisenberg, Lisa, and Katy Hall. 101 Ghost Jokes; GrL: 4-up; RdL: 2

Fife, Dale. Follow That Ghost; GrL: 2-4; RdL: 2

Fife, Dale. Sesame Seed Snatchers; GrL: 4-6; RdL: 4

Fleischman, Sid. McBroom Tells a Lie; GrL: 2-5; RdL: 4

Foley, June. Love By Any Other Name; GrL: 7-up; RdL: 3

Foley, Louise Munro. Tackle 22; GrL: 2-4; RdL: 2

Gardiner, John Reynolds. Top Secret; GrL: 4-6; RdL: 3

Giff, Patricia Reilly. Ronald Morgan Goes to Bat; GrL: 3-4; RdL: 1

Giff, Patricia Reilly. Say "Cheese"; GrL: 4-6; RdL: 2

Giff, Patricia Reilly. Watch Out, Ronald Morgan; GrL: 1-3; RdL: 1

Gilson, Jamie. Double Dog Dare; GrL: 3-6; RdL: 2

Haas, Dorothy. Secret Life of Dilly McBean; GrL: 5-7; RdL: 4

Hall, Katy, and Lisa Eisenberg. Buggy Riddles; GrL: 2-4; RdL: 1

Handford, Martin. Find Waldo Now; GrL: 4-6; RdL: 6

Hunting-Fiction

Ice Hockey-Fiction

Ice Skating
Kalb, Jonah. Easy Ice Skating Book;
GrL: 2-5; RdL: 2

Ice Skating-Fiction
Levy, Elizabeth. Cold As Ice; GrL: 6-9;
RdL: 4

Imagination-Fiction
Bulla, Clyde Robert. Chalk Box Kid;
GrL: 2-4; RdL: 2
Hoff, Syd. Horse in Harry's Room; GrL:
1-4; RdL: 1

Immigration-Fiction
Bunting, Eve. How Many Days to
America? A Thanksgiving Story; GrL:
1-4; RdL: 2

Independence-Fiction
Bunting, Eve. If I Asked You, Would You
Stay?; GrL: 7-up; RdL: 3
Claypool, Jane. Jasmine Finds Love;
GrL: 6-up; RdL: 3

Individuality-Fiction
Conford, Ellen. And This Is Laura; GrL:
4-7; RdL: 4

Inner City Life-Fiction
Levoy, Myron. Shadow Like a Leopard,
A; GrL: 6-up; RdL: 3
Myers, Walter Dean. Hoops; GrL: 7-up;
RdL: 4
Wagner, Jane. J.T.; GrL: 3-6; RdL: 4

Insects-Fiction
Hall, Katy, and Lisa Eisenberg. Buggy
Riddles; GrL: 2-4; RdL: 1

Israel-Fiction
Chaikin, Miriam. Aviva's Piano; GrL: 3-
4; RdL: 3

Jealousy-Fiction
Cole, Johanna. Missing Tooth; GrL: 1-3;
RdL: 1

Jews-Fiction
Arrick, Fran. Chernowitz!; GrL: 6-up;
RdL: 5

Jobs
Alexander, Sue. Finding Your First Job;
GrL: 9-up; RdL: 3

Jokes and Riddles
Kessler, Leonard. Old Turtle's Riddle and
Joke Book; GrL: 1-3; RdL: 1
Rosenbloom, Joseph. Ridiculous Nicholas
Riddle Book; GrL: 2-6; RdL: Varies
Rosenbloom, Joseph. Spooky Riddles and
Jokes; GrL: 3-6; RdL: Varies

Karate-Fiction
Hiller, B.B. Karate Kid; GrL: 5-up;
RdL: 5

Kennedy, John Fitzgerald
Donnelly, Judy. Who Shot the President?
The Death of John F. Kennedy; GrL: 3-
6; RdL: 4

Kidnapping-Fiction
Sharmat, Marjorie Weinman. Get Rich
Mitch!; GrL: 4-6; RdL: 3

Latchkey Children-Fiction
Bunting, Eve. Is Anybody There?; GrL:
4-8; RdL: 3

Leadership-Fiction
Bunting, Eve. Skateboard Four; GrL: 4-7;
RdL: 3

Legends
Blassingame, Wyatt. Pecos Bill Rides a
Tornado; GrL: 2-5; RdL: 2
De Leeuw, Adele. Paul Bunyan Finds a
Wife; GrL: 2-5; RdL: 2
Schwartz, Alvin. Scary Stories to Tell in
the Dark; GrL: 4-6; RdL: 3

Lincoln, Abraham
Colver, Anne. Abraham Lincoln; GrL: 4-
6; RdL: 2

Loneliness-Fiction

Bulla, Clyde Robert. Chalk Box Kid;
GrL: 2-4; RdL: 2

Rylant, Cynthia. Henry and Mudge: The
First Book; GrL: 1-3; RdL: 1

Savitz, Harriet May. Swimmer; GrL: 4-6;
RdL: 3

Love-Fiction

Byars, Betsy. Beans on the Roof; GrL: 2-
4; RdL: 2

Magic

Kraske, Robert. Magicians Do Amazing
Things; GrL: 3-6; RdL: 2

Magic-Fiction

Avi. Bright Shadow; GrL: 5-9; RdL: 2

Avi. No More Magic; GrL: 3-6; RdL: 3

Chew, Ruth. Do-It-Yourself Magic; GrL:
2-5; RdL: 3

Chew, Ruth. No Such Thing as a Witch;
GrL: 4-6; RdL: 2

Dubowski, Cathy East. Pretty Good
Magic; GrL: 1-3; RdL: 2

Magicians-Biography

Edwards, Anne. Great Houdini; GrL: 4-6;
RdL: 3

Magicians-Fiction

Levy, Elizabeth. Case of the Gobbling
Squash; GrL: 2-5; RdL: 3

Levy, Elizabeth. Running Out of Magic
with Houdini; GrL: 4-6; RdL: 3

Malcolm X

Adoff, Arnold. Malcolm X; GrL: 3-6;
RdL: 3

Maturation

Cole, Joanna. Asking about Sex and
Growing Up; GrL: 5-up; RdL: Varies

Meaning of Life-Fiction

Hall, Lynn. If Winter Comes; GrL: 6-up;
RdL: 5

Mentally Handicapped-Fiction

Bates, Betty. Love Is Like Peanuts; GrL:
6-up; RdL: 3

Byars, Betsy. Summer of the Swans;
GrL: 6-9; RdL: 6

Middle Ages-Fiction

Skurzynski, Gloria. Minstrel in the Tower;
GrL: 2-4; RdL: 2

Minutemen-Fiction

Benchley, Nathaniel. Sam the Minuteman;
GrL: 1-4; RdL: 2

Mischief-Fiction

Seuss, Dr. Cat in the Hat; GrL: 1-3;
RdL: 1

Models

Simon, Seymour. Paper Airplane Book;
GrL: 3-6; RdL: 4

Money-Fiction

Christian, Mary Blount. Mysterious Case
Case; GrL: 3-5; RdL: 4

Conford, Ellen. Job for Jenny Archer;
GrL: 2-4; RdL: 3

Quackenbush, Robert. Piet Potter's First
Case; GrL: 3-5; RdL: 3

Monkeys-Fiction

Clifford, Eth. Harvey's Marvelous
Monkey Mystery; GrL: 4-6; RdL: 4

Monsters

Bulla, Clyde Robert. My Friend the
Monster; GrL: 2-5; RdL: 1

Cohen, Daniel. Monsters of Star Trek;
GrL: 7-up; RdL: 7

Parish, Peggy. No More Monsters for
Me!; GrL: 1-4; RdL: 1

Platt, Kin. Frank and Stein and Me; GrL:
5-9; RdL: 2

Stevenson, Drew. Case of the Wandering
Werewolf; GrL: 4-6; RdL: 3

Thorne, Ian. Frankenstein; GrL: 2-6;
RdL: 3

Motorcycle Races
Hallum, Red. Kookie Rides Again; GrL: 2-6; RdL: 4

Motorcycles
Radlauer, Edward. Motorcycle Mania; GrL: 2-6; RdL: 1

Movie Stars-Fiction
Shaw, Diana. Gone Hollywood; GrL: 6-9; RdL: 3

Movies
Aylesworth, Thomas G. Movie Monsters; GrL: 3-6; RdL: 3
Blinn, William. Brian's Song; GrL: 6-up; RdL: 2
Hiller, B.B. Karate Kid; GrL: 5-up; RdL: 5
Thorne, Ian. Frankenstein; GrL: 2-6; RdL: 3

Moving-Fiction
Blume, Judy. Tiger Eyes; GrL: 6-up; RdL: 3
Greene, Carol. Jenny Summer; GrL: 2-4; RdL: 2
Hurwitz, Johanna. Aldo Applesauce; GrL: 3-5; RdL: 3
Lowry, Lois. Anastasia Again!; GrL: 4-6; RdL: 3
Slote, Alfred. Moving In; GrL: 4-6; RdL: 3
Wolkoff, Judie. Wally; GrL: 4-6; RdL: 4

Murder
Madison, Arnold. Great Unsolved Cases; GrL: 6-up; RdL: 3

Murder-Fiction
Bennett, Jay. Dangling Witness; GrL: 7-up; RdL: 2
Bennett, Jay. Dark Corridor; GrL: 9-up; RdL: 2
Bennett, Jay. Pigeon; GrL: 7-up; RdL: 4
Bennett, Jay. Shadows Offstage; GrL: 7-up; RdL: 2

Giff, Patricia Reilly. Suspect; GrL: 7-up; RdL: 1
Nixon, Joan Lowery. Seance; GrL: 6-up; RdL: 3

Mysteries
Abels, Harriet Sheffer. Haunted Motorcycle Shop; GrL: 5-8; RdL: 3
Adler, David A. Cam Jansen & the Mystery of the Stolen Diamonds; GrL: 2-4; RdL: 2
Adler, David A. Fourth Floor Twins and the Sand Castle Contest; GrL: 2-4; RdL: 2
Avi. No More Magic; GrL: 3-6; RdL: 3
Avi. Wolf Rider: a Tale of Terror; GrL: 7-up; RdL: 3
Bennett, Jay. Dangling Witness; GrL: 7-up; RdL: 2
Bennett, Jay. Dark Corridor; GrL: 9-up; RdL: 2
Bennett, Jay. Pigeon; GrL: 7-up; RdL: 4
Bennett, Jay. Say Hello to the Hit Man; GrL: 7-up; RdL: 4
Bennett, Jay. Shadows Offstage; GrL: 7-up; RdL: 2
Bennett, Jay. Skeleton Man; GrL: 7-up; RdL: 2
Berends, Polly. Case of the Elevator Duck; GrL: 4-6; RdL: 3
Bunting, Eve. Is Anybody There?; GrL: 4-8; RdL: 3
Bunting, Eve. Skate Patrol; GrL: 2-4; RdL: 2
Cameron, Ann. Julian, Secret Agent; GrL: 1-3; RdL: 2
Christian, Mary Blount. Mysterious Case Case; GrL: 3-5; RdL: 4
Christopher, Matt. Red-Hot Hightops; GrL: 6-9; RdL: 3
Christopher, Matt. Tackle without a Team; GrL: 6-9; RdL: 2
Clifford, Eth. Harvey's Marvelous Monkey Mystery; GrL: 4-6; RdL: 4
Conford, Ellen. Case for Jenny Archer, A; GrL: 2-4; RdL: 3

Eisenberg, Lisa. Killer Music; GrL: 6-up; RdL: 2

Fife, Dale. Follow That Ghost; GrL: 2-4; RdL: 2

Fife, Dale. Sesame Seed Snatchers; GrL: 4-6; RdL: 4

Fleischman, Paul. Phoebe Danger, Detective in the Case of the Two-Minute Cough; GrL: 4-5; RdL: 3

Fleischman, Sid. Bloodhound Gang in the Case of the Secret Message; GrL: 4-6; RdL: 4

Giff, Patricia Reilly. Have You Seen Hyacinth Macaw?; GrL: 4-6; RdL: 3

Giff, Patricia Reilly. Powder Puff Puzzle; GrL: 2-4; RdL: 1

Giff, Patricia Reilly. Suspect; GrL: 7-up; RdL: 1

Gorman, Carol. Chelsey and the Green-Haired Kid; GrL: 7-9; RdL: 5

Greene, Janice. Flight of the Sparrow; GrL: 9-up; RdL: 4

Haas, Dorothy. To Catch a Crook; GrL: 4-6; RdL: 3

Hildick, E.W. Case of the Wandering Weathervanes; GrL: 4-6; RdL: 4

Howe, James. Stage Fright; GrL: 6-up; RdL: 4

Landon, Lucinda. Meg Mackintosh and the Case of the Missing Babe Ruth Baseball; GrL: 2-4; RdL: 2

Law, Carol Russell. Case of the Weird Street Firebug; GrL: 4-6; RdL: 3

Levy, Elizabeth. Case of the Gobbling Squash; GrL: 2-5; RdL: 3

Levy, Elizabeth. Cold As Ice; GrL: 6-9; RdL: 4

Levy, Elizabeth. Dani Trap; GrL: 6-up; RdL: 3

Levy, Elizabeth. Something Queer at the Ballpark; GrL: 2-4; RdL: 2

Lorimer, Janet. Time's Reach; GrL: 9-up; RdL: 3

Madison, Arnold. Great Unsolved Cases; GrL: 6-up; RdL: 3

Montgomery, Elizabeth R. Mystery of the Boy Next Door; GrL: 2-4; RdL: 1

Nixon, Joan Lowery. Seance; GrL: 6-up; RdL: 3

Parish, Peggy. Clues in the Woods; GrL: 1-4; RdL: 2

Quackenbush, Robert. Piet Potter's First Case; GrL: 3-5; RdL: 3

Sharmat, Marjorie Weinman. Nate the Great and the Fishy Prize; GrL: 2-4; RdL: 3

Sharmat, Marjorie Weinman. Nate the Great and the Snowy Trail; GrL: 2-4; RdL: 2

Shaw, Diana. Gone Hollywood; GrL: 6-9; RdL: 3

Simon, Seymour. Einstein Anderson, Science Sleuth; GrL: 4-6; RdL: 3

Sobol, Donald J. Encyclopedia Brown Boy Detective; GrL: 3-6; RdL: 3

Stevenson, Drew. Case of the Wandering Werewolf; GrL: 4-6; RdL: 3

Timmons, Stan. Black Gold Conspiracy; GrL: 9-up; RdL: 4

White, Robb. Deathwatch; GrL: 6-up; RdL: 4

Williams, Jan. Danny Dunn, Scientific Detective; GrL: 4-7; RdL: 3

New York City-Fiction

Danziger, Paula. Remember Me to Harold Square; GrL: 6-up; RdL: 2

Nuclear War-Fiction

Hall, Lynn. If Winter Comes; GrL: 6-up; RdL: 5

Obesity-Fiction

Blume, Judy. Blubber; GrL: 4-6; RdL: 3

DeClements, Barthe. Nothing's Fair in Fifth Grade; GrL: 4-6; RdL: 3

Olympics-Fiction

Kessler, Leonard. On Your Mark, Get Set, Go!; GrL: K-4; RdL: 1

Optimism-Fiction

Chaikin, Miriam. Aviva's Piano; GrL: 3-4; RdL: 3

Pregnancy-Fiction
Eyerly, Jeannette. Someone to Love Me;
GrL: 7-up; RdL: 3

Prejudice-Fiction
Arrick, Fran. Chernowitz!; GrL: 6-up;
RdL: 5
Blume, Judy. Blubber; GrL: 4-6; RdL: 3

Presidents
Donnelly, Judy. Who Shot the President?
The Death of John F. Kennedy; GrL: 3-
6; RdL: 4

Presidents-Biography
Colver, Anne. Abraham Lincoln; GrL: 4-
6; RdL: 2
Heilbroner, Joan. Meet George
Washington; GrL: 4-6; RdL: 2

Puzzles
Handford, Martin. Find Waldo Now;
GrL: 4-6; RdL: 6
Handford, Martin. Where's Waldo?; GrL:
3-6; RdL: 3
Sobol, Donald J. Encyclopedia Brown
Boy Detective; GrL: 3-6; RdL: 3

Puzzles-Fiction
Simon, Seymour. Einstein Anderson,
Science Sleuth; GrL: 4-6; RdL: 3

Quicksand
DePaola, Tomie. Quicksand Book; GrL:
K-3; RdL: 2

Rabbits-Fiction
Dubowski, Cathy East. Pretty Good
Magic; GrL: 1-3; RdL: 2
Parish, Peggy. Too Many Rabbits; GrL:
1-3; RdL: 1

Rare Animals
Leslie-Melville, Betty. Daisy Rothschild
Giraffe That Lives with Me; GrL: 4-8;
RdL: 6

Recreation
Gray, William R. Camping Adventure;
GrL: 3-6; RdL: 2
Handford, Martin. Find Waldo Now;
GrL: 4-6; RdL: 6
Hanford, Martin. Where's Waldo?; GrL:
3-6; RdL: 3
Kraske, Robert. Magicians Do Amazing
Things; GrL: 3-6; RdL: 2
Petersen, David. Airplanes; GrL: 3-6;
RdL: 3
Peterson, John. How to Write Codes and
Send Secret Messages; GrL: 3-5;
RdL: 2

Refugees-Fiction
Bunting, Eve. How Many Days to
America? A Thanksgiving Story; GrL:
1-4; RdL: 2

Relationships
Vedral, Joyce L. Opposite Sex Is Driving
Me Crazy; GrL: 6-up; RdL: 5

Relationships-Fiction
Cole, Brock. Goats; GrL: 6-up; RdL: 2

Remarriage-Fiction
Pevsner, Stella. Sister of the Quints; GrL:
6-9; RdL: 2
Slote, Alfred. Friend Like That, A; GrL:
4-6; RdL: 3

Reproduction
Cole, Joanna. My Puppy Is Born; GrL: 1-
4; RdL: 2

Reptiles
Lauber, Patricia. Snakes Are Hunters;
GrL: 1-4; RdL: 2

Responsibility-Fiction
Bunting, Eve. Ghosts of Departure Point;
GrL: 5-up; RdL: 2
Davis, Jenny. Sex Education; GrL: 7-9;
RdL: 2

Rhyme

LeSiego. Wacky Wednesday; GrL: 1-3; RdL: 1

Seuss, Dr. Cat in the Hat Comes Back; GrL: 1-3; RdL: 1

Seuss, Dr. Cat in the Hat; GrL: 1-3; RdL: 1

Riddles

Adler, David A. Dinosaur Princess and Other Prehistoric Riddles; GrL: 2-5; RdL: 2

Eisenberg, Lisa, and Katy Hall. 101 Ghost Jokes; GrL: 4-up; RdL: 2

Hall, Katy, and Lisa Eisenberg. Buggy Riddles; GrL: 2-4; RdL: 1

Kessler, Leonard. Old Turtle's Riddle and Joke Book; GrL: 1-3; RdL: 1

Rosenbloom, Joseph. Ridiculous Nicholas Riddle Book; GrL: 2-6; RdL: Varies

Rosenbloom, Joseph. Spooky Riddles and Jokes; GrL: 3-6; RdL: Varies

Ride, Sally

Blacknall, Carolyn. Sally Ride: America's First Woman in Space; GrL: 6-9; RdL: 6

Robots-Fiction

Slote, Alfred. C.O.L.A.R.: A Tale of Outer Space; GrL: 4-6; RdL: 4

Slote, Alfred. Omega Station; GrL: 3-6; RdL: 3

Yolen, Jane. Robot and Rebecca: The Mystery of the Code-Carrying Kids; GrL: 3-6; RdL: 4

Rock Music-Fiction

Franklin, Lance. Double Play; GrL: 6-up; RdL: 5

Strasser, Todd. Rock 'N' Roll Nights; GrL: 7-up; RdL: 5

Rock Musicians-Biography

Eichhorn, Dennis P. Springsteen; GrL: 6-up; RdL: 4

Rock Musicians-Fiction

Eisenberg, Lisa. Killer Music; GrL: 6-up; RdL: 2

Roller Skating-Fiction

Bunting, Eve. Skate Patrol; GrL: 2-4; RdL: 2

Romance

Avi. Romeo and Juliet: Together (and Alive) at Last; GrL: 5-8; RdL: 2

Bates, Betty. Love Is Like Peanuts; GrL: 6-up; RdL: 3

Bunting, Eve. Girl in the Painting; GrL: 6-up; RdL: 5

Bunting, Eve. Karen Kepplewhite Is the World's Best Kisser; GrL: 4-6; RdL: 2

Cavanna, Betty. Banner Year; GrL: 7-up; RdL: 4

Claypool, Jane. Jasmine Finds Love; GrL: 6-up; RdL: 3

Conford, Ellen. If This Is Love, I'll Take Spaghetti; GrL: 6-up; RdL: 4

Conford, Ellen. Strictly for Laughs; GrL: 6-up; RdL: 4

Conford, Ellen. Things I Did for Love; GrL: 6-up; RdL: 4

Danziger, Paula. Remember Me to Harold Square; GrL: 6-up; RdL: 2

Foley, June. Love By Any Other Name; GrL: 7-up; RdL: 3

Levy, Elizabeth. Cold As Ice; GrL: 6-9; RdL: 4

Levy, Elizabeth. Dani Trap; GrL: 6-up; RdL: 3

Martin, Ann M. Just a Summer Romance; GrL: 6-9; RdL: 3

Mazer, Harry. Girl of His Dreams; GrL: 7-up; RdL: 2

Mazer, Norma Fox. Up in Seth's Room; GrL: 6-up; RdL: 3

Strasser, Todd. Rock 'N' Roll Nights; GrL: 7-up; RdL: 5

Roosevelt, Eleanor

Goodsell, Jane. Eleanor Roosevelt; GrL: 2-4; RdL: 2

Runaways-Fiction

Angell, Judie. Dear Lola or How to Build Your Own Family; GrL: 4-6; RdL: 4

Bunting, Eve. If I Asked You, Would You Stay?; GrL: 7-up; RdL: 3

Running-Fiction

Cowen, Eve. Catch the Sun; GrL: 9-up; RdL: 5

Marzollo, Jean. Red Ribbon Rosie; GrL: 2-4; RdL: 3

Mazer, Harry. Girl of His Dreams; GrL: 7-up; RdL: 2

Platt, Kin. Brogg's Brain; GrL: 6-10; RdL: 2

Scavenger Hunts-Fiction

Danziger, Paula. Remember Me to Harold Square; GrL: 6-up; RdL: 2

Schools-Fiction

Adler, David A. Jeffrey's Ghost and the Fifth-Grade Dragon; GrL: 3-5; RdL: 2

Avi. Romeo and Juliet: Together (and Alive) at Last; GrL: 5-8; RdL: 2

Blume, Judy. Blubber; GrL: 4-6; RdL: 3

Blume, Judy. Freckle Juice; GrL: 2-4; RdL: 3

Bunting, Eve. Girl in the Painting; GrL: 6-up; RdL: 5

Byars, Betsy. Burning Questions of Bingo Brown; GrL: 5-up; RdL: 5

Curtis, Philip. Invasion of the Brain Sharpeners; GrL: 4-6; RdL: 3

Danziger, Paula. Cat Ate My Gymsuit; GrL: 6-9; RdL: 5

DeClements, Barthe. Nothing's Fair in Fifth Grade; GrL: 4-6; RdL: 3

Delton, Judy. Only Jody; GrL: 4-6; RdL: 3

Etrat, Jonathan. Aliens for Breakfast; GrL: 3-4; RdL: 3

Gardiner, John Reynolds. Top Secret; GrL: 4-6; RdL: 3

Gilson, Jamie. Double Dog Dare; GrL: 3-6; RdL: 2

Greenwald, Sheila. Valentine Rosy; GrL: 3-5; RdL: 3

Haas, Dorothy. To Catch a Crook; GrL: 4-6; RdL: 3

Heide, Florence Parry. Banana Twist; GrL: 4-6; RdL: 4

Kassem, Lou. Middle School Blues; GrL: 5-8; RdL: 2

Kline, Suzy. Herbie Jones; GrL: 3-4; RdL: 3

Kline, Suzy. Herbie Jones and the Class Gift; GrL: 3-5; RdL: 3

Park, Barbara. Almost Starring Skinnybones; GrL: 3-6; RdL: 3

Sharmat, Marjorie Weinman. Getting Something on Maggie Marmelstein; GrL: 3-6; RdL: 3

Science

Branley, Franklyn Mansfield. Eclipse: Darkness in Daytime; GrL: 1-4; RdL: 2

DePaola, Tomie. Quicksand Book; GrL: K-3; RdL: 2

Greene, Carol. Astronauts; GrL: 3-6; RdL: 3

Markle, Sandra. Science Mini-Mysteries; GrL: 4-6; RdL: Varies

Morris, Robert A. Seahorse; GrL: 2-4; RdL: 1

Shaw, Evelyn. Alligator; GrL: 2-4; RdL: 2

Simon, Seymour. Einstein Anderson, Science Sleuth; GrL: 4-6; RdL: 3

Science Fiction

Berry, James R. Dar Tellum: Stranger from a Distant Planet; GrL: 4-6; RdL: 4

Clark, Margaret Goff. Barney and the UFO; GrL: 4-7; RdL: 4

Curtis, Philip. Invasion of the Brain Sharpeners; GrL: 4-6; RdL: 3

DeWeese, Gene. Nightmares from Space; GrL: 6-12; RdL: 2

Etrat, Jonathan. Aliens for Breakfast; GrL: 3-4; RdL: 3

Gardiner, John Reynolds. Top Secret; GrL: 4-6; RdL: 3

Haas, Dorothy. Secret Life of Dilly McBean; GrL: 5-7; RdL: 4

Sex Roles-Fiction
Cynthia, Blair. Marshmallow
Masquerade; GrL: 6-up; RdL: 4
Gutman, Bill. Smitty; GrL: 6-up; RdL: 4

Sexuality
Vedral, Joyce L. Opposite Sex Is Driving
Me Crazy; GrL: 6-up; RdL: 5

Sexuality-Fiction
Davis, Jenny. Sex Education; GrL: 7-9;
RdL: 2
Mazer, Norma Fox. Up in Seth's Room;
GrL: 6-up; RdL: 3

Sexually Transmitted Diseases
Nourse, Alan E. Teen Guide to Safe Sex;
GrL: 6-up; RdL: 6

Ships
Donnelly, Judy. Titanic Lost and Found;
GrL: 2-4; RdL: 2

Short Stories
Cohen, Daniel. Headless Roommate and
Other Tales of Terror; GrL: 7-up;
RdL: 5
Conford, Ellen. If This Is Love, I'll Take
Spaghetti; GrL: 6-up; RdL: 4
Lobel, Arnold. Frog and Toad Together;
GrL: K-3; RdL: 1
Rotsler, William. Star Trek III: Short
Stories; GrL: 6-up; RdL: 6
Schwartz, Alvin. In a Dark, Dark Room
and Other Scary Stories; GrL: K-3;
RdL: 1
Sobol, Donald J. Encyclopedia Brown
Boy Detective; GrL: 3-6; RdL: 3

Sibling Rivalry-Fiction
Pevsner, Stella. And You Give Me a Pain,
Elaine; GrL: 4-6; RdL: 3

Sign Language
Patterson, Francine. Koko's Kitten; GrL:
2-6; RdL: 3

Single-Parent Families-Fiction
Bonham, Frank. Durango Street; GrL: 8-
up; RdL: 6
Cleary, Beverly. Dear Mr. Henshaw; GrL:
5-8; RdL: 5
Greene, Shep. Boy Who Drank Too
Much; GrL: 6-up; RdL: 2
Savitz, Harriet May. Swimmer; GrL: 4-6;
RdL: 3
Slote, Alfred. Moving In; GrL: 4-6;
RdL: 3
Smith, Alison. Help! There's a Cat
Washing in Here!; GrL: 4-6; RdL: 4

Skateboarding-Fiction
Bunting, Eve. Skateboard Four; GrL: 4-7;
RdL: 3

Skiing-Fiction
Cowen, Eve. High Escape; GrL: 9-up;
RdL: 4

Snakes
Lauber, Patricia. Snakes Are Hunters;
GrL: 1-4; RdL: 2

Soccer
Devaney, John. Secrets of the Super
Athletes: Soccer; GrL: 6-up; RdL: 6
Dickmeyer, Lowell A. Soccer Is for Me;
GrL: 2-4; RdL: 2

Soccer-Fiction
Kessler, Leonard. Old Turtle's Soccer
Team; GrL: 1-4; RdL: 1

Spacemen-Fiction
Harding, Lee. Fallen Spaceman; GrL: 2-
5; RdL: 3

Spies
Laymon, Richard. Cobra; GrL: 9-up; RdL: 5
Timmons, Stan. Black Gold Conspiracy;
GrL: 9-up; RdL: 4

Spies-Fiction
Bromley, Dudley. Balloon Spies; GrL: 7-
up; RdL: 4

Girard, Ken. Double Exposure; GrL: 9-up; RdL: 5

Sports

Aaseng, Nathan. Baseball: It's Your Team; GrL: 6-up; RdL: 7

Aaseng, Nathan. Football: It's Your Team; GrL: 6-up; RdL: 7

Appel, Marty. First Book of Baseball; GrL: 2-6; RdL: 4

Barrett, Norman S. Racing Cars; GrL: 3-6; RdL: 4

Berger, Melvin. Photo Dictionary of Football; GrL: 6-12; RdL: 5

Broekel, Ray. Football; GrL: 3-6; RdL: 2

Burchard, Marshall. Terry Bradshaw; GrL: 3-6; RdL: 4

Cluck, Bob. Baserunning; GrL: 6-9; RdL: 6

Cluck, Bob. Hitting; GrL: 6-9; RdL: 6

Cluck, Bob. Shortstop; GrL: 6-9; RdL: 6

Devaney, John. Secrets of the Super Athletes: Soccer; GrL: 6-up; RdL: 6

Dickmeyer, Lowell A. Soccer Is for Me; GrL: 2-4; RdL: 2

Dolan, Edward F. Great Moments in the Super Bowl; GrL: 4-8; RdL: 3

Greene, Carol. I Can Be a Baseball Player; GrL: 1-4; RdL: 2

Gutman, Bill. Pro Football's Record Breakers; GrL: 6-up; RdL: 6

Hallum, Red. Kookie Rides Again; GrL: 2-6; RdL: 4

Jones, Betty Millsaps. Wonder Women of Sports; GrL: 4-8; RdL: 3

Kalb, Jonah. Easy Baseball Book; GrL: 2-5; RdL: 2

Kalb, Jonah. Easy Hockey Book; GrL: 2-5; RdL: 2

Kalb, Jonah. Easy Ice Skating Book; GrL: 2-5; RdL: 2

Madden, John. First Book of Football; GrL: 6-up; RdL: 4

Radlauer, Edward. Motorcycle Mania; GrL: 2-6; RdL: 1

Sullivan, George. Center; GrL: 6-9; RdL: 6

Sullivan, George. Pitcher; GrL: 3-6; RdL: 4

Weber, Bruce. Bruce Weber's Inside Pro Football 1988; GrL: 6-up; RdL: 5

Sports-Fiction

Christopher, Matt. Hit-Away Kid; GrL: 3-5; RdL: 3

Christopher, Matt. Red-Hot Hightops; GrL: 6-9; RdL: 3

Cowen, Eve. High Escape; GrL: 9-up; RdL: 4

Franklin, Lance. Takedown; GrL: 6-up; RdL: 4

Kessler, Leonard. Old Turtle's Baseball Stories; GrL: 1-3; RdL: 1

Kessler, Leonard. On Your Mark, Get Set, Go!; GrL: K-4; RdL: 1

Kline, Suzy. Herbie Jones and the Monster Ball; GrL: 3-5; RdL: 3

O'Connor, Dick. Foul Play; GrL: 9-up; RdL: 4

Platt, Kin. Brogg's Brain; GrL: 6-10; RdL: 2

Rice, Earle. Fear on Ice; GrL: 9-up; RdL: 4

Slote, Alfred. Hotshot; GrL: 3-6; RdL: 2

Sportsmanship-Fiction

Kessler, Leonard. Old Turtle's Soccer Team; GrL: 1-4; RdL: 1

Springsteen, Bruce

Eichhorn, Dennis P. Springsteen; GrL: 6-up; RdL: 4

Star Trek (TV Series)

Cohen, Daniel. Monsters of Star Trek; GrL: 7-up; RdL: 7

Rotsler, William. Star Trek III: Short Stories; GrL: 6-up; RdL: 6

Stepfamilies-Fiction

Walter, Mildred Pitts. Mariah Loves Rock; GrL: 4-6; RdL: 3

Stepmothers-Fiction

Pevsner, Stella. Sister of the Quints; GrL: 6-9; RdL: 2

Grade Index

All Ages
Larrick, Nancy. Cats Are Cats

Preschool - 3
Berenstain, Stan. Bike Lesson
Eisler, Colin. Cats Know Best

K-3
Byars, Betsy. Golly Sisters Go West
DePaola, Tomie. Quicksand Book
Kuklin, Susan. Taking My Cat to the Vet
Lobel, Arnold. Frog and Toad Together
Roy, Ron. What Has Ten Legs and Eats
Corn Flakes?
Schwartz, Alvin. In a Dark, Dark Room and
Other Scary Stories

K-4
Kessler, Leonard. On Your Mark,
Get Set, Go!
Lopshire, Robert. How to Make Snop
Snappers and Other Fine Things
Viorst, Judith. Tenth Good Thing About
Barney

Grades 1-3
Cameron, Ann. Julian's Glorious Summer
Cameron, Ann. Julian, Secret Agent
Cole, Joanna. Missing Tooth
Dubowski, Cathy East. Pretty Good Magic
Giff, Patricia Reilly. Watch Out, Ronald
Morgan
Hayward, Linda. Hello, House!
Hoff, Syd. Stanley
Kessler, Leonard. Old Turtle's Baseball
Stories
Kessler, Leonard. Old Turtle's Riddle and
Joke Book
King, P.E. Down on the Funny Farm
Krensky, Stephen. Lionel in the Fall
LeSiego. Wacky Wednesday
Marzollo, Jean, and Claudio Marzollo. Jed
and the Space Bandits
Parish, Peggy. Too Many Rabbits

Rylant, Cynthia. Henry and Mudge in the
Green Time
Rylant, Cynthia. Henry and Mudge: The
First Book
Rylant, Cynthia. Henry and Mudge: Under
the Yellow Moon
Seuss, Dr. Cat in the Hat Comes Back
Seuss, Dr. Cat in the Hat

Grades 1-4
Benchley, Nathaniel. Sam the Minuteman
Branley, Franklyn Mansfield. Eclipse:
Darkness in Daytime
Bunting, Eve. How Many Days to America?
A Thanksgiving Story
Cole, Joanna. My Puppy Is Born
Gauch, Patricia Lee. Aaron and the Green
Mountain Boys
Greene, Carol. I Can Be a Baseball Player
Hoff, Syd. Horse in Harry's Room
Hopkins, Lee Bennett, ed. More Surprises
Hopkins, Lee Bennett, ed. Surprises
Kessler, Leonard. Old Turtle's Soccer Team
Lauber, Patricia. Snakes Are Hunters
Parish, Peggy. Clues in the Woods
Parish, Peggy. No More Monsters for Me!

Grades 1-6
Silverstein, Shel. Light in the Attic, A

Grades 2-4
Adler, David A. Cam Jansen & the Mystery
of the Stolen Diamonds
Adler, David A. Fourth Floor Twins and the
Sand Castle Contest
Bare, Colleen Stanley. To Love a Dog
Blume, Judy. Freckle Juice
Bulla, Clyde Robert. Chalk Box Kid
Bunting, Eve. Skate Patrol
Byars, Betsy. Beans on the Roof
Cameron, Ann. More Stories Julian Tells
Cameron, Ann. Stories Julian Tells
Carlson, Natalie Savage. Ghost in the
Lagoon

Conford, Ellen. Case for Jenny Archer, A
Conford, Ellen. Job for Jenny Archer
Dickmeyer, Lowell A. Soccer Is for Me
Donnelly, Judy. Titanic Lost and Found
Fife, Dale. Follow That Ghost
Foley, Louise Munro. Tackle 22
Giff, Patricia Reilly. Powder Puff Puzzle
Goodsell, Jane. Eleanor Roosevelt
Greene, Carol. Jenny Summer
Hall, Katy, and Lisa Eisenberg. Buggy
    Riddles
Landon, Lucinda. Meg Mackintosh and the
    Case of the Missing Babe Ruth Baseball
Levy, Elizabeth. Something Queer at the
    Ballpark
Malone, Mary. Annie Sullivan
Marzollo, Jean. Red Ribbon Rosie
Montgomery, Elizabeth R. Mystery of the
    Boy Next Door
Morris, Robert A. Seahorse
Prelutsky, Jack. What I Did Last Summer
Sharmat, Marjorie Weinman. Nate the Great
    and the Fishy Prize
Sharmat, Marjorie Weinman. Nate the Great
    and the Snowy Trail
Shaw, Evelyn. Alligator
Skurzynski, Gloria. Minstrel in the Tower
Van Woerkom, Dorothy. Becky and the Bear
Yolen, Jane. Commander Toad and the
    Space Pirates

Grades 2-5
Adler, David A. Dinosaur Princess and
    Other Prehistoric Riddles
Blassingame, Wyatt. Pecos Bill Rides a
    Tornado
Bulla, Clyde Robert. My Friend the Monster
Chew, Ruth. Do-It-Yourself Magic
De Leeuw, Adele. Paul Bunyan Finds a Wife
Fleischman, Sid. McBroom Tells a Lie
Glendinning, Sally. Doll: Bottle-Nosed
    Dolphin
Harding, Lee. Fallen Spaceman
Kalb, Jonah. Easy Baseball Book
Kalb, Jonah. Easy Hockey Book
Kalb, Jonah. Easy Ice Skating Book
Levy, Elizabeth. Case of the Gobbling
    Squash

Manes, Stephen. Boy Who Turned into a TV
    Set
Peterson, John. Littles' Surprise Party
Stevens, Carla. Trouble for Lucy

Grades 2-6
Appel, Marty. First Book of Baseball
Hallum, Red. Kookie Rides Again
Hart, Angela. Dogs
Patterson, Francine. Koko's Kitten
Radlauer, Edward. Motorcycle Mania
Rosenbloom, Joseph. Ridiculous Nicholas
    Riddle Book
Thorne, Ian. Frankenstein
Tripp, Valerie. Molly Saves the Day: A
    Summer Story

Grades 3-4
Chaikin, Miriam. Aviva's Piano
Donnelly, Judy. Tut's Mummy: Lost...and
    Found
Etrat, Jonathan. Aliens for Breakfast
Giff, Patricia Reilly. Ronald Morgan Goes
    to Bat
Hooks, William H. Pioneer Cat
Kline, Suzy. Herbie Jones

Grades 3-5
Adler, David A. Jeffrey's Ghost and the
    Fifth-Grade Dragon
Anderson, LaVere. Mary McLeod Bethune:
    Teacher with a Dream
Bason, Lillian. Those Foolish Molboes
Christian, Mary Blount. Mysterious Case
    Case
Christopher, Matt. Hit-Away Kid
Greenwald, Sheila. Valentine Rosy
Hurwitz, Johanna. Aldo Applesauce
Kline, Suzy. Herbie Jones and the Class Gift
Kline, Suzy. Herbie Jones and the Monster
    Ball
Levy, Elizabeth. Frankenstein Moved In on
    the Fourth Floor
Luenn, Nancy. Unicorn Crossing
Miles, Betty. Secret Life of the Underwear
    Champ
Morressy, John. Drought on Ziax II
Orgel, Doris. Whiskers Once and Always

Peterson, John. How to Write Codes and Send Secret Messages

Quackenbush, Robert. Piet Potter's First Case

Tapp, Kathy Kennedy. Den 3 Meets the Jinx

Grades 3-6

Adoff, Arnold. Malcolm X

Avi. No More Magic

Aylesworth, Thomas G. Movie Monsters

Barrett, Norman S. Racing Cars

Blume, Judy. Tales of a Fourth Grade Nothing

Broekel, Ray. Football

Bulla, Clyde Robert. Pirate's Promise

Burchard, Marshall. Terry Bradshaw

Corbett, Scott. Great McGoniggle Rides Shotgun

Donnelly, Judy. Who Shot the President? The Death of John F. Kennedy

Gilson, Jamie. Double Dog Dare

Gray, William R. Camping Adventure

Greene, Carol. Astronauts

Hall, Lynn. Captain: Canada's Flying Pony

Handford, Martin. Where's Waldo?

Harris, Robie H. Rosie's Double Dare

Kalb, Jonah. Goof That Won the Pennant

Kraske, Robert. Magicians Do Amazing Things

Latham, Jean Lee. Elizabeth Blackwell: Pioneer Woman Doctor

Levine, Ellen. Secret Missions: Four True Life Stories

Monjo, Ferdinand N. Vicksburg Veteran

Park, Barbara. Almost Starring Skinnybones

Petersen, David. Airplanes

Rockwell, Thomas. How to Eat Fried Worms

Roop, Peter. Keep the Lights Burning, Abbie

Rosenbloom, Joseph. Spooky Riddles and Jokes

Roy, Ron. Nightmare Island

Sharmat, Marjorie Weinman. Getting Something on Maggie Marmelstein

Simon, Seymour. Paper Airplane Book

Slote, Alfred. Hotshot

Slote, Alfred. Omega Station

Sobol, Donald J. Encyclopedia Brown Boy Detective

Sullivan, George. Pitcher

Wagner, Jane. J.T.

Walker, Alice. Langston Hughes, American Poet

Wallace, Bill. Danger on Panther Peak

Yolen, Jane. Robot and Rebecca: The Mystery of the Code-Carrying Kids

Grades 3-8

Sobol, Donald J. Encyclopedia Brown's 3rd Record Book of Weird & Wonderful Facts

Grades 3 and up

Krementz, Jill. How It Feels to Be Adopted

Krementz, Jill. How It Feels When a Parent Dies

Krementz, Jill. How It Feels When Parents Divorce

Grades 4-5

Fleischman, Paul. Phoebe Danger, Detective in the Case of the Two-Minute Cough

Grades 4-6

Adams, Barbara Johnston. Picture Life of Bill Cosby

Angell, Judie. Dear Lola or How to Build Your Own Family

Avi. Man from the Sky

Berends, Polly. Case of the Elevator Duck

Berry, James R. Dar Tellum: Stranger from a Distant Planet

Blume, Judy. Blubber

Boutis, Victoria. Katy Did It

Brown, Drollene P. Sybil Rides for Independence

Bunting, Eve. Karen Kepplewhite Is the World's Best Kisser

Byars, Betsy. Good-bye, Chicken Little

Chew, Ruth. No Such Thing as a Witch

Cleary, Beverly. Socks

Clifford, Eth. Harvey's Marvelous Monkey Mystery

Clifford, Eth. Help! I'm a Prisoner in the Library

Clifford, Eth. I Never Wanted to Be Famous

Colver, Anne. Abraham Lincoln

Curtis, Philip. Invasion of the Brain Sharpeners

Grades 4-7

Grades 4-8

Reading Level Index

Grade 1

Berenstain, Stan. Bike Lesson, The

Bulla, Clyde Robert. My Friend the Monster

Byars, Betsy. Golly Sisters Go West, The

Cole, Joanna. Missing Tooth, The

Eisler, Colin. Cats Know Best

Giff, Patricia Reilly. Powder Puff Puzzle, The

Giff, Patricia Reilly. Ronald Morgan Goes to Bat

Giff, Patricia Reilly. Suspect

Giff, Patricia Reilly. Watch Out, Ronald Morgan

Hall, Katy, and Lisa Eisenberg. Buggy Riddles

Hayward, Linda. Hello, House!

Hoff, Syd. Horse in Harry's Room, The

Kessler, Leonard. Old Turtle's Baseball Stories

Kessler, Leonard. Old Turtle's Riddle and Joke Book

Kessler, Leonard. Old Turtle's Soccer Team

Kessler, Leonard. On Your Mark, Get Set, Go!

King, P.E. Down on the Funny Farm

LeSieg, Theo. Wacky Wednesday

Lobel, Arnold. Frog and Toad Together

Lopshire, Robert. How to Make Snop Snappers and Other Fine Things

Montgomery, Elizabeth R. Mystery of the Boy Next Door, The

Morris, Robert A. Seahorse

Parish, Peggy. No More Monsters for Me!

Parish, Peggy. Too Many Rabbits

Radlauer, Edward. Motorcycle Mania

Rylant, Cynthia. Henry and Mudge in the Green Time

Rylant, Cynthia. Henry and Mudge: The First Book

Rylant, Cynthia. Henry and Mudge: Under the Yellow Moon

Schwartz, Alvin. In a Dark, Dark Room and Other Scary Stories

Seuss, Dr. Cat in the Hat Comes Back, The

Seuss, Dr. Cat in the Hat, The

Yolen, Jane. Commander Toad and the Space Pirates

Grade 2

Adler, David A. Cam Jansen & the Mystery of the Stolen Diamonds

Adler, David A. Dinosaur Princess and Other Prehistoric Riddles, The

Adler, David A. Fourth Floor Twins and the Sand Castle Contest, The

Adler, David A. Jeffrey's Ghost and the Fifth-Grade Dragon

Avi. Bright Shadow

Avi. Devil's Race

Avi. Man from the Sky

Avi. Romeo and Juliet: Together (and Alive) at Last

Bare, Colleen Stanley. To Love a Dog

Benchley, Nathaniel. Sam the Minuteman

Bennett, Jay. Dangling Witness, The

Bennett, Jay. Dark Corridor, The

Bennett, Jay. Shadows Offstage

Bennett, Jay. Skeleton Man, The

Blassingame, Wyatt. Pecos Bill Rides a Tornado

Blinn, William. Brian's Song

Branley, Franklyn Mansfield. Eclipse: Darkness in Daytime

Broekel, Ray. Football

Bulla, Clyde Robert. Chalk Box Kid, The

Bulla, Clyde Robert. Pirate's Promise

Bunting, Eve. Ghosts of Departure Point, The

Bunting, Eve. How Many Days to America? A Thanksgiving Story

Bunting, Eve. Karen Kepplewhite Is the World's Best Kisser

Bunting, Eve. Skate Patrol, The

Van Woerkom, Dorothy. Becky and the Bear

Viorst, Judith. Tenth Good Thing About Barney, The

Wallace, Bill. Danger on Panther Peak

Grade 3

Abels, Harriet Sheffer. Haunted Motorcycle Shop, The

Adams, Barbara Johnston. Picture Life of Bill Cosby, The

Adoff, Arnold. Malcolm X

Alexander, Sue. Finding Your First Job

Anderson, LaVere. Mary McLeod Bethune: Teacher with a Dream

Avi. No More Magic

Avi. Wolf Rider: A Tale of Terror

Aylesworth, Thomas G. Movie Monsters

Bason, Lillian. Those Foolish Molboes

Bates, Betty. Love Is Like Peanuts

Bauer, Marion Dane. On My Honor

Berends, Polly. Case of the Elevator Duck, The

Blume, Judy. Blubber

Blume, Judy. Freckle Juice

Blume, Judy. It's Not the End of the World

Blume, Judy. Tales of a Fourth Grade Nothing

Blume, Judy. Tiger Eyes

Boutis, Victoria. Katy Did It

Bunting, Eve. If I Asked You, Would You Stay?

Bunting, Eve. Is Anybody There?

Bunting, Eve. Janet Hamm Needs a Date for the Dance

Bunting, Eve. Skateboard Four

Bunting, Eve. Someone Is Hiding on Alcatraz Island

Butterworth, W.E. LeRoy and the Old Man

Cameron, Ann. More Stories Julian Tells

Cameron, Ann. Stories Julian Tells, The

Chaikin, Miriam. Aviva's Piano

Chew, Ruth. Do-It-Yourself Magic

Christopher, Matt. Hit-Away Kid, The

Christopher, Matt. Red-Hot Hightops

Claypool, Jane. Jasmine Finds Love

Conford, Ellen. Case for Jenny Archer, A

Conford, Ellen. Job for Jenny Archer

Curtis, Philip. Invasion of the Brain Sharpeners

Davidson, Margaret. Story of Benjamin Franklin, Amazing American, The

DeClements, Barthe. Nothing's Fair in Fifth Grade

Delton, Judy. Only Jody

Dolan, Edward F. Great Moments in the Super Bowl

Duncan, Lois. I Know What You Did Last Summer

Edwards, Anne. Great Houdini, The

Etrat, Jonathan. Aliens for Breakfast

Eyerly, Jeannette. Someone to Love Me

Fleischman, Paul. Phoebe Danger, Detective in the Case of the Two-Minute Cough

Foley, June. Love By Any Other Name

Franchere, Ruth. Cesar Chavez

Gardiner, John Reynolds. Top Secret

Giff, Patricia Reilly. Have You Seen Hyacinth Macaw?

Glendinning, Sally. Doll: Bottle-Nosed Dolphin

Greene, Carol. Astronauts

Greenwald, Sheila. Valentine Rosy

Haas, Dorothy. To Catch a Crook

Hall, Lynn. Captain: Canada's Flying Pony

Handford, Martin. Where's Waldo?

Harding, Lee. Fallen Spaceman, The

Hart, Angela. Dogs

Hurwitz, Johanna. Aldo Applesauce

Jones, Betty Millsaps. Wonder Women of Sports

Kline, Suzy. Herbie Jones

Kline, Suzy. Herbie Jones and the Class Gift

Kline, Suzy. Herbie Jones and the Monster Ball

Latham, Jean Lee. Elizabeth Blackwell: Pioneer Woman Doctor

Law, Carol Russell. Case of the Weird Street Firebug, The

Levoy, Myron. Shadow Like a Leopard, A

Levy, Elizabeth. Case of the Gobbling Squash, The

Levy, Elizabeth. Dani Trap

Levy, Elizabeth. Running Out of Magic with Houdini

Lorimer, Janet. Time's Reach

Lowry, Lois. Anastasia Again!

Luenn, Nancy. Unicorn Crossing

Madison, Arnold. Great Unsolved Cases

Malone, Mary. Annie Sullivan

Manes, Stephen. Hooples' Haunted House, The

Martin, Ann M. Just a Summer Romance

Marzollo, Jean. Red Ribbon Rosie

Mazer, Harry. When the Phone Rang

Mazer, Norma Fox. Up in Seth's Room

Morressy, John. Drought on Ziax II, The

Morressy, John. Humans of Ziax II, The

Nixon, Joan Lowery. Seance, The

O'Connor, Jim, and Jane O'Connor. Ghost in Tent 19, The

Park, Barbara. Almost Starring Skinnybones

Park, Barbara. Don't Make Me Smile

Patterson, Francine. Koko's Kitten

Paulsen, Gary. Tracker

Petersen, David. Airplanes

Pevsner, Stella. And You Give Me a Pain, Elaine

Quackenbush, Robert. Piet Potter's First Case

Rockwell, Thomas. How to Eat Fried Worms

Rockwell, Thomas. How to Fight a Girl

Rodgers, Mary. Freaky Friday

Roy, Ron. Nightmare Island

Savitz, Harriet May. Swimmer

Schwartz, Alvin. Scary Stories to Tell in the Dark

Sharmat, Marjorie Weinman. Get Rich Mitch!

Sharmat, Marjorie Weinman. Getting Something on Maggie Marmelstein

Sharmat, Marjorie Weinman. Nate the Great and the Fishy Prize

Shaw, Diana. Gone Hollywood

Simon, Seymour. Einstein Anderson, Science Sleuth

Singer, Marilyn. It Can't Hurt Forever

Slote, Alfred. Friend Like That, A

Slote, Alfred. Moving In

Slote, Alfred. Omega Station

Sobol, Donald J. Encyclopedia Brown Boy Detective

Sommer-Bodenburg, Angela. My Friend the Vampire

Sorrels, Roy. New Life, A

Stevens, Carla. Trouble for Lucy

Stevenson, Drew. Case of the Wandering Werewolf, The

Tapp, Kathy Kennedy. Den 3 Meets the Jinx

Thorne, Ian. Frankenstein

Tripp, Valerie. Molly Saves the Day: A Summer Story

Walter, Mildred Pitts. Mariah Loves Rock

Williams, Jan. Danny Dunn, Scientific Detective

Grade 4

Angell, Judie. Dear Lola or How to Build Your Own Family

Anonymous. Go Ask Alice

Appel, Marty. First Book of Baseball, The

Barrett, Norman S. Racing Cars

Bennett, Jay. Pigeon, The

Bennett, Jay. Say Hello to the Hit Man

Berry, James R. Dar Tellum: Stranger from a Distant Planet

Bromley, Dudley. Balloon Spies

Brown, Drollene P. Sybil Rides for Independence

Brown, Fern G. Teen Guide to Childbirth

Burchard, Marshall. Terry Bradshaw

Byars, Betsy. Good-bye, Chicken Little

Cavanna, Betty. Banner Year

Christian, Mary Blount. Mysterious Case Case, The

Clark, Margaret Goff. Barney and the UFO

Clifford, Eth. Harvey's Marvelous Monkey Mystery

Clifford, Eth. I Never Wanted to Be Famous

Cohen, Daniel. Restless Dead, The

Conford, Ellen. And This Is Laura

Conford, Ellen. If This Is Love, I'll Take Spaghetti

Conford, Ellen. Strictly for Laughs

Conford, Ellen. Things I Did for Love, The

Cowen, Eve. High Escape

Cynthia, Blair. Marshmallow Masquerade

Dolan, Edward F. Great Mysteries of the Air

Donnelly, Judy. True-Life Treasure Hunts

Donnelly, Judy. Who Shot the President? The Death of John F. Kennedy

Eichhorn, Dennis P. Springsteen

Fife, Dale. North of Danger

Fife, Dale. Sesame Seed Snatchers, The

Fleischman, Sid. Bloodhound Gang in the Case of the Secret Message, The

Fleischman, Sid. McBroom Tells a Lie

Franklin, Lance. Takedown

Gauch, Patricia Lee. Thunder at Gettysburg

Greene, Janice. Flight of the Sparrow

Gutman, Bill. Smitty

Haas, Dorothy. Secret Life of Dilly McBean, The

Hallum, Red. Kookie Rides Again

Heide, Florence Parry. Banana Twist

Hildick, E.W. Case of the Wandering Weathervanes, The

Howe, James. Stage Fright

Hurwitz, Johanna. Adventures of Ali Baba Bernstein, The

Kalb, Jonah. Goof That Won the Pennant, The

Kibbe, Pat. Hocus-Pocus Dilemma, The

Levine, Ellen. Secret Missions: Four True Life Stories

Levy, Elizabeth. Cold As Ice

Levy, Elizabeth. Frankenstein Moved In on the Fourth Floor

Lewis, Marjorie. Wrongway Applebaum

Madden, John. First Book of Football, The

Manes, Stephen. Boy Who Turned into a TV Set, The

Moore, Allan. British Are Coming, The

Myers, Walter Dean. Hoops

O'Connor, Dick. Foul Play

Park, Barbara. Skinnybones

Peterson, John. Littles' Surprise Party, The

Pfeffer, Susan Beth. Kid Power

Renner, Beverly Hollett. Hideaway Summer, The

Rice, Earle. Fear on Ice

Robinet, Harriette Gillem. Ride the Red Cycle

Shura, Mary Francis. Barkley Street Six-Pack, The

Simon, Seymour. Paper Airplane Book, The

Slote, Alfred. C.O.L.A.R.: A Tale of Outer Space

Slote, Alfred. My Trip to Alpha I

Smith, Alison. Help! There's a Cat Washing in Here!

Smith, Doris Buchanan. Taste of Blackberries, A

Sullivan, George. Pitcher

Timmons, Stan. Black Gold Conspiracy, The

Wagner, Jane. J.T.

Wagner, Robin S. Sarah T.: Portrait of a Teen-Age Alcoholic

Walker, Alice. Langston Hughes, American Poet

White, Robb. Deathwatch

Wolkoff, Judie. Wally

Wright, Betty Ren. Pike River, The

Yolen, Jane. Robot and Rebecca: The Mystery of the Code-Carrying Kids, The

Grade 5

Adler, C.S. Split Sisters

Arnosky, Jim. Gray Boy

Arrick, Fran. Chernowitz!

Berger, Melvin. Photo Dictionary of Football, The

Bunting, Eve. Girl in the Painting, The
Byars, Betsy. Burning Questions of Bingo Brown, The
Cleary, Beverly. Dear Mr. Henshaw
Cohen, Daniel. Headless Roommate and Other Tales of Terror, The
Cowen, Eve. Catch the Sun
Danziger, Paula. Cat Ate My Gymsuit, The
DuPrau, Jeanne. Golden God
Franklin, Lance. Double Play
Girard, Ken. Double Exposure
Gorman, Carol. Chelsey and the Green-Haired Kid
Hall, Lynn. If Winter Comes
Hallowell, Tommy. Out of Bounds
Hiller, B.B. Karate Kid, The
Laymon, Richard. Cobra, The
Mazer, Harry. Snow Bound
Mazer, Harry. War on Villa Street, The
Milton, Hilary. Mayday! Mayday!
Strasser, Todd. Rock 'N' Roll Nights
Thomas, Jane Resh. Comeback Dog, The
Vedral, Joyce L. Opposite Sex Is Driving Me Crazy, The
Weber, Bruce. Bruce Weber's Inside Pro Football 1988

Grade 6
Blacknall, Carolyn. Sally Ride: America's First Woman in Space
Bonham, Frank. Durango Street
Byars, Betsy. Summer of the Swans
Cluck, Bob. Baserunning
Cluck, Bob. Hitting
Cluck, Bob. Shortstop
Devaney, John. Secrets of the Super Athletes: Soccer
Gutman, Bill. Pro Football's Record Breakers
Handford, Martin. Find Waldo Now
Hinton, S.E. Taming the Star Runner
Hinton, S.E. That Was Then, This Is Now
Leslie-Melville, Betty. Daisy Rothschild, The Giraffe That Lives with Me

Nourse, Alan E. Teen Guide to Birth Control
Nourse, Alan E. Teen Guide to Safe Sex
Rotsler, William. Star Trek III: Short Stories
Sullivan, George. Center

Grade 7
Aaseng, Nathan. Baseball: It's Your Team
Aaseng, Nathan. Football: It's Your Team
Cohen, Daniel. Monsters of Star Trek, The
Paulsen, Gary. Hatchet

No Words
Ames, Lee J. Draw Fifty Monsters, Creeps, Superheroes, etc.

Varies
Cole, Joanna. Asking about Sex and Growing Up
Hopkins, Lee Bennett, ed. More Surprises
Hopkins, Lee Bennett, ed. Surprises
Krementz, Jill. How It Feels to Be Adopted
Krementz, Jill. How It Feels When a Parent Dies
Krementz, Jill. How It Feels When Parents Divorce
Larrick, Nancy. Cats Are Cats
Markle, Sandra. Science Mini-Mysteries
Prelutsky, Jack. What I Did Last Summer
Rosenbloom, Joseph. Ridiculous Nicholas Riddle Book
Rosenbloom, Joseph. Spooky Riddles and Jokes
Silverstein, Shel. Light in the Attic, A
Sobol, Donald J. Encyclopedia Brown's 3rd Record Book of Weird & Wonderful Facts